CONFLICT MASTERY
Questions to Guide You
Workbook

CINNIE NOBLE

2015
CINERGY™ Coaching

CINERGY™ Coaching
Phone: 416-686-4247
Toll free (Canada & US): 1-866-335-6466
Fax: 416-686-9178
Email: info@cinergycoaching.com
Web: http://www.cinergycoaching.com

Copy editing and proofreading: Francine Geraci
Production editing: Laura Bast, WordsWorth Communications
Text and cover design: Tara Wells, WordsWorth Communications
Cover image: Blurino/500px Prime

ISBN 978-0-9877394-3-8

The topic and question pages may be reproduced to enhance your use of the workbook.

With this well-written book, Cinnie Noble emphasizes the magic of asking questions to help our clients (and ourselves) to reflect on different ways of looking at and being in conflict. Clarifying, possibility, caring, compassionate, and thoughtful questions are aimed at helping clients to re-script the narratives that define and justify their actions. This book offers both practical and thought-provoking ideas for all professionals working with conflicts. Reading *Conflict Mastery: Questions to Guide You* gives a sense of being in the presence of a gifted, engaging, enthusiastic, and inspiring conflict management coach and mediator.

—Dr. Fredrike Bannink, MDR, Master of Dispute Resolution & International Full Certified ADR Mediator, author of *Handbook of Solution-Focused Conflict Management* and *1001 Solution-Focused Questions: Handbook for Solution-Focused Interviewing*

***

With inquiry being at the heart of effective coaching, Cinnie Noble's book provides powerful questions, together with comprehensive explanations on a range of topics, toward the aim of moving forward any client in conflict. Keep this book close in order to transform virtually any conflict situation into a platinum opportunity for growth, learning, and productivity.

—Rey Carr, PhD, CEO, Peer Resources

***

The path to productive conflict is about having the right questions, not the right answers. *Conflict Mastery: Questions to Guide You* provides both profound insights and practical tools, and should be required reading for anyone trying to build a high-performing team.

—Liane Davey, PhD, NYT bestselling author of *You First: Inspire Your Team to Grow Up, Get Along, and Get Stuff Done*

***

This latest Noble effort is equally suited for coaches, students, teachers, mediation professionals, neophytes, or any folks just trying to understand their conflict behaviors. Eschewing high-falutin' academic gibberish as well as saccharine self-help babble, it's an easy and clear read, with lots of useful takeaways. Chock-a-block with insightful questions and practical tools, this book is a veritable Swiss army knife for the conflict-curious—without the stabbiness.

—Brad Heckman, CEO, New York Peace Institute

***

Cinnie Noble is a global leader in the field of conflict management. In her latest book, she shares the most accessible secret of her success: How to ask the right question at the right time and in the right manner in order to enable people to discover how a radically different approach to their disputes can change the course of their lives. Cinnie's use of mindful questions before, during, and after conflict is absolutely brilliant, illuminating, and ground-breaking.

—Ralph H. Kilmann, PhD, co-author of the *Thomas-Kilmann Conflict Mode Instrument* (TKI) and CEO of Kilmann Diagnostics

***

In *Conflict Mastery: Questions to Guide You*, Cinnie provides practical tips and methods that guide us through the dark and often terrifying quagmire of disagreement. The techniques she offers are deceptively simple; in reality, they are powerful, practical, and effective tools. As well, her questions encourage thoughtful reflection that leads to constructive action. This is a wonderful book—as insightful and intelligent as it is relevant and practical.

—Michael Lang, Professor of Conflict Resolution and former Editor-in Chief, *Mediation Quarterly*

***

This book belongs in the permanent collection of everyone who wants to fine-tune their reactions or get a better handle on a conflict. Open almost any section before, during, or after conflict and you'll find the perfect question to give you greater insight. Cinnie Noble has taken the art of inquiry to a truly masterful level.

—Tammy Lenski, author, *The Conflict Pivot*

***

Conflict Mastery: Questions to Guide You provides a comprehensive understanding of conflict management. Written in an easy-to-access style, it enables individuals to consider such aspects as preparation and analysis, as well as action. This book is well worth reading, and no one will come away disappointed, given the learning it contains.

—Gladeana McMahon, International Transformational Coach, author and Chair Emeritus of the Association for Coaching UK

***

World-renowned conflict management coach, Cinnie Noble, delivers a gift in *Conflict Mastery: Questions to Guide You*. She shares powerful, thought-provoking questions on a wide range of conflict issues. By answering her questions, you'll find yourself drawn from conflict misery to conflict mastery!

—Craig Runde, Director, Center for Conflict Dynamics and co-author of *Becoming a Conflict Competent Leader*

***

Cinnie Noble skillfully guides readers through effective reflection in *Conflict Mastery: Questions to Guide You*. Empathy, understanding, and insight—the bedrock of effectively handling conflict—are born from asking good questions. Readers will benefit enormously from reading her excellent book.

—Alan Tidwell, Georgetown University

***

Cinnie Noble, doyenne of Conflict Management Coaching, brings her deep experience and unique mastery to *Conflict Mastery: Questions to Guide You*. This book takes readers on an inspiring journey that has the power to change their lives forever. A must-read for coaches, it contains numerous questions that will exponentially expand your capacity to coach effectively in conflict situations. This book is indeed a masterpiece!

—Adria Trowhill, Dean, Adler Coaching Certificate Program

***

Cinnie Noble's new book, *Conflict Mastery: Questions to Guide You*, provides the reader with overview, insight, and practical approaches to working with conflict. Based on her sound understanding of the structure of conflict, the book is designed to support increasing awareness through the use of powerful, focused questions. Cinnie's systematic approach guides the reader through a process that builds insight and emotional intelligence. I recommend this book to all coaches looking for a powerful framework for dealing with their own conflicts or for assisting their clients to move beyond conflict situations.

—Karen Tweedie, PCC, Partner, Point Ahead Australia,
Systemic Coaching Specialist

*To the memory of
my colleague and friend,
Jennifer Lynch*

Contents

CHAPTER THREE
During Conflict, 97

Acknowledgments

Above all, my deepest appreciation goes to my assistant, Laureen McNeill, who gives special meaning to the word team. Without her, many of the dreams I have envisioned over the last 20 years would not have come to fruition. To my coaching and mediation clients—thank you for trusting me. You are awesome and teach me every day about the magic of questions, that we have the choice to be who and how we want to be in conflict, and that we have the power to make it a positive experience.

To my colleagues and **CINERGY**® Coaching trainers and coach-mentors far and wide—thank you from the bottom of my heart for all you do and for supporting me with your thoughtfulness, caring, and wisdom. Sincere thanks go to my very skillful and conscientious editor, Francine Geraci, and to Paula Pike, Jim Lyons, Tara Wells, and Laura Bast of WordsWorth Communications for your diligence and creativity. To my dear and wonderful family and friends, I am so grateful for your continuing support and love.

Sometimes

Sometimes
if you move carefully
through the forest

breathing
like the ones
in the old stories

who could cross
a shimmering bed of dry leaves
without a sound,

you come
to a place
whose only task

is to trouble you
with tiny
but frightening requests

conceived out of nowhere
but in this place
beginning to lead everywhere.

requests to stop what
you are doing right now,
and

to stop what you
are becoming
while you do it,

questions
that can make
or unmake
a life,

questions
that have patiently
waited for you,

questions that have no right
to go away.

— David Whyte*

* Printed with permission from Many Rivers Press, www.davidwhyte.com, *Everything is Waiting for You*, 2007.

CHAPTER ONE

Important Considerations About Questions, Conflict, and Conflict Mastery

What Questions Do

Philosophers, leaders—spiritual, religious, organizational, and others—psychologists, therapists, teachers, and lawyers have all used questions since time immemorial to inspire, challenge, encourage dialogue, and elicit information. Coaches, mediators, trainers, and group facilitators also use well-crafted and open-ended questions to do the same, and to stretch thinking, motivate visioning, and build awareness. What is more, questions are used to uncover and clarify truths, attributions, and thoughts and feelings that lie dormant within us.

In my work as a lawyer, mediator, and conflict management coach, I have been intrigued by the power of questions for a long time. I am fascinated when they open up new and different perspectives. I marvel at questions that plant seeds that then germinate when least expected. I like that questions help to reappraise and reframe viewpoints. I highly value questions that reveal new pathways that increase insights and engender possibilities that were not previously contemplated.

My interest in the power of questions evolved exponentially in my work as a coach, and I have had the joy of reading a number of great books written about the art of inquiry.[1] As with other forms of coaching, asking powerful questions is a core competency that is meant to facilitate clients' self-discovery—an integral step in any effort to make positive changes in our lives.

During the course of developing a coaching framework specifically designed for helping people to find their way through conflict and to strengthen their skills in this area, I discovered experientially what and how questions inspire clients to think in different ways about themselves and their disputes. As a practitioner, I continue to see how certain questions serve to broaden clients' reflections about their perspectives on their conflicts and on the other person's, too.

I regularly witness how some questions help clients distance themselves from their negative interactions. In doing so, I listen as they rethink their assumptions and re-script the narratives that initially defined and justified their actions. I hear, too, how "clarifying" questions unlock answers that help people navigate the ambiguities and uncertainties of their disputes. I literally watch "possibility" questions spark positivity that ignites at times of pessimism and despair.

More happens, too. I hear how "caring" questions facilitate clients' self-empathy and empathy for the person with whom they are in dispute. I observe how such questions open up thought and heart space—enabling people to think and feel broader and deeper. Compassionate and thoughtful questions also help people move along a continuum from reaction to reflection—shifting away from their emotional pain and counterproductive thoughts to ultimately contemplating a range of possible options and plans for moving forward. Along the way it is noticeable, as well, how the experience of being in conflict shifts for the better.

In addition, I observe durable changes in clients' relationship to themselves and others as a consequence of the questions and answers they explore about ways to optimize their potential for becoming conflict intelligent. I hear them loosen their grip on time-worn conflict habits with the concentrated effort to improve the way they interact. I see how "envisioning" questions help clients explore ways to approach discord more constructively, caringly, and confidently. I watch as clients no longer shy away from identifying and addressing things that provoke them. And I listen to people let go of self-limiting beliefs about their ability to engage in conflict.

With all this, I have come to truly appreciate the magic of questions. I became inspired to compile the types of queries I have found that increase my clients' self-awareness in their efforts to manage their disputes more effectively and to develop and strengthen conflict intelligence and mastery (concepts to be discussed later in this chapter). This book concentrates, then, on reflective questions as tools to facilitate self-examination—a major step in the process of getting there. It is based on my blog, *ConflictMastery*™ *Quest(ions)*.[2]

What Is Conflict?

There are many definitions of conflict, and the content of this book is about the sorts of interpersonal disputes that negatively affect us and take a toll on our personal and professional relationships and everyday lives. Some of us may use terms like argument, quarrel, disagreement, altercation, controversy, fight, or personality conflict to describe them. (In any case, this book is *not* about war, domestic violence, or other forms of physical and emotional abuse or attack.) Here are some relevant definitions and components of conflict:

Any situation in which interdependent people have apparently incompatible interests, goals, principles or feelings.[3]

A condition between two interdependent people in which one or both feel angry at the other and perceive the other as being at fault.[4]

... simply the sound made by cracks in a system; regardless of whether the system is personal, relational, familial, organizational, social, economic or political.[5]

... when we experience a threat to our desires, expected patterns of interaction, and our sense of right and wrong ... .[6]

Considering these and other definitions, it is suggested that the main components of interpersonal conflict are as follows:

- At least one person perceives that there is something amiss between her or him and another person.

- Incompatibilities exist about how at least one person views her or his own perspectives, goals, interests, expectations, actions, words, or ways of communicating, as opposed to the other person's.

- The person (or persons) who perceives discord experiences negative and unsettling emotions that prevail and preoccupy—sometimes for protracted periods of time.

- Fault-finding is often part of the interrelational dynamic that emerges.

- External or internal physical reactions, or both, commonly occur for the person (or persons) experiencing discord.

- There is a desire to act on the conflict situation.[7]

Ten Premises of the Content of This Book

The premises of this book's content—along with the definitions and components of conflict just described—form the frame and foundation for the types of questions asked. They are as follows:

1. Interpersonal conflict is a normal and inevitable part of interacting with others in our personal and professional lives.

2. Many of us have things we want to improve about the way we manage and engage in conflict. We do not have all the answers about how to do so because, to give only one possible reason, we do not know which questions to ask.

3. Conflict is often due to perceived challenges or threats to aspects of ourselves such as our needs, values, identities, beliefs, expectations, hopes, interests, and well-being.

4. We have developed habits about how we engage in conflict, and not all of them serve us well. Typically, we first learn these habits from the dynamics we observe and participate in, in our families of origin. As we grow up, we also learn ways to manage interpersonal conflict from our teachers, peers, colleagues, life and business partners, and from our cultures, religions, communities, workplaces, and other sources. It seems, however, that trial and error are our main teachers as we develop our own unique patterns of communicating

and interacting when we encounter conflict. As a consequence, the questions we ask ourselves, and how we answer them, reflect our individual ways of being in relationship to ourselves and with others in the wide range of potentially discordant contexts that emerge in our day-to-day lives.

5. Peace with others begins with peace within ourselves. Though it is not possible to change others, we have the ability to change the way we engage in conflict—to unlearn habits that are not effective, and to learn new ways of being. To do so requires focus, motivation, time, the ability to reflect and empathize with ourselves and others, and the desire and willingness to improve.

6. We have choices about what to change and strengthen regarding the way we manage and engage in conflict. For instance, we have choices about how we want to be and be perceived, how we interact and communicate with the other person, and how we respond.

7. Inquiry that invites us to understand, among other things, our values, needs, hopes, and expectations—and those of others—helps us become more attuned with ourselves and with them, too. Increasing our awareness in these and other ways also contributes to the ability to explore choices and changes that are consistent with how and who we prefer to be before, during, and after conflict.

8. When we choose to change what we are in charge of—ourselves—we influence a change in the paradigm with those with whom we are in conflict. That is, it takes just one person to influence a shift in the nature of our interactions.

9. When we are in dispute with others, we are essentially cooperating with and are complicit in the conflict dynamic that evolves. This means we are participants and share the responsibility in the potential and real deterioration of the communications and relationship. Doing or saying nothing equates to participating, just as active involvement does.

10. When we are provoked and become upset because of conflictual interactions, it is helpful to engage our prefrontal cortex and calm the amygdala—to be able to gain perspective and emotional distance from the dynamic. Questions that ask us to reflect on new and different ways of viewing and feeling about our experiences help facilitate that. They create new connections, and they assist us to think more clearly and creatively, to recognize what is real and not imagined, to make decisions, to problem solve, to gain increased awareness and insights, and to consider, understand, and empathize with the other person's perspective, too.

Conflict Mastery

As part of this book's title and throughout, the phrase "conflict mastery" is used, and the meaning I ascribe to it is defined here.

Essentially, when we achieve conflict mastery we accept the inevitability of interpersonal conflict and want to engage in it effectively because we care about ourselves, our relationships, and our hopes, values, needs, and other aspects of our humanness. Conflict mastery is about developing the ability to participate with confidence and compassion in conversations and situations in which we perceive challenges to these and other parts of ourselves. It means acknowledging that we have the choice to approach conflict and the other person in thoughtful, respectful, and responsive ways.

What is more, conflict mastery means we have gained the knowledge and skills to understand and analyze conflict dynamics. This entails contemplating and exploring not only what is going on for ourselves when we react to stimuli that provoke us. We also pay attention to, and consider what may be going on with, the other person. It is about listening to and acknowledging her or his views, even if she or he says or does things that provoke us. We contemplate how we may be contributing to the discord in ways that adversely affect the other person and the course of the conflict. We take responsibility for doing so and our part in the interaction.

Conflict mastery is about exploring the opportunities that exist within the discord and choosing to facilitate constructive and positive conflict, as discussed below. It also refers to having the ability and courage to be proactive about our conflicts. We make the time to think out what has happened or is happening to see whether things become clearer in our mind and settled in our heart before responding to others who say and do things that trigger adverse reactions in us. We instill trust and make it safe for others to raise difficult matters with us. Similarly, we think out what to say, and how to say it, before raising contentious matters. When we act with conflict mastery, we remain cognizant of what we want as an outcome for our relationships, and govern ourselves accordingly.

Further, when we are conflict masterful we accept that we do not have to agree on everything, and that—at a minimum—hearing and paying attention to what our differences are enriches an understanding of what is important to each other. We respond rather than react. We reflect before we respond. We do not operate on assumptions and judgment. We do not attribute fault, motives, character and personality traits, and so on. We think about what we are thinking and feeling. We regulate our emotions. When we are conflict masterful, we remain aware at all times—not only when we are in conflict—that how we treat others reflects on our self-respect and how we show up in the world. We strive to gain increased self-awareness to be able to interact with dignity, respect, and humility.

When we are conflict masterful, we acknowledge when and how conflict affects our health, and actively attend to our healing. We learn from our mistakes, are grateful for the learning, and apply it in future disputes. We are resilient. We apologize when we offend others. We forgive. We know, too, when the most beneficial step for all concerned is to walk away, and we do so with grace.

In this book you will also read the phrase "conflict intelligence." Conflict intelligence is, in my view, as important to develop as emotional, social, and other intelligences needed to lead fulfilling, happy, and meaningful lives, to work productively, and to interact in positive and mutually respectful ways.

Being conflict intelligent refers to developing proficiency—the knowledge, skills, and ability—needed to engage in and manage our interpersonal conflicts and disputes effectively. When that is achieved and demonstrated, conflict mastery is reached. I think of being conflict intelligent, then, as what we develop and become with learning and practice. Conflict mastery is what we do that successfully reflects what we have learned.

Positive Conflict

For many, it is difficult to think of the word "conflict" qualified by the adjective "positive." However, many of us in the conflict management field—coaches, mediators, and other alternative dispute resolution practitioners—approach our work as peacebuilders with the knowledge that interpersonal conflict provides an opportunity to learn and grow. This is consistent with the concepts of conflict intelligence and mastery, and one of the outcomes of developing them. More specifically, what makes conflict positive?

The meaning suggested here is that positive conflict is about understanding and accepting the notion that our interpersonal challenges present us with opportunities to acknowledge the breadth and depth of our own and one another's humanness, and to discover what is important to each of us and why. It is that interpersonal conflict also provides the opportunity to better understand and empathize with ourselves and those with whom we live and work. By doing so, we have the chance to consider what it takes to reconcile our differences and improve the relationship, if that is something we want. Conflict also helps us to get in touch with and express what we need for our well-being, and to be with and stay connected to others.

Further, positive conflict is *not* about having to be right and making others wrong. It is about a mindset that accepts our differences without having or needing to find fault or attribute blame. It is about seeing whether we are able to bridge the gap that exists between our disparate views and ways of interacting with one another—to be in a space and place we prefer to be.

Rather than causing us to reject other people's views and feelings, positive conflict means exploring, recognizing, and building on common ground to the extent that it is possible. It means discovering where we may stand together to share and understand each other's perspectives, and the impact of what is being experienced as a consequence of our incompatibilities. By making an effort to see whether we are able to do this, the potential is higher for resolving and mending our differences and disconnections.

Another aspect of positive conflict in this regard is that discussions undertaken with positive intent provide the possibility for attaining a stronger grasp of the dynamics of the interaction and the ability to determine what is needed to move forward. This includes expressing our perspective truthfully and transparently, and making the space for the other person to express thoughts and feelings that want out, too.

The concept of positive conflict supports the view that when we choose to communicate with the other person in our conflicts in curious, responsive, and respectful ways, we become more attuned to them and to ourselves. When we are willing to listen, we become increasingly able to expand our thinking. When we then share what we perceive is happening and its impact, we open up the dialogue that liberates our ability to check out assumptions, consider mutually acceptable solutions, improve how we interact, and reduce the tension and stress.

Compatible with the concept of conflict intelligence and mastery, striving to make interpersonal conflict a positive experience entails being open to, and grateful for, discovering what can be learned and gained from the dispute.

Positive conflict also means the humbling acceptance that we are human beings, after all. We are not going to like, applaud, or appreciate everything that other humans say and do, and we, too, have our foibles. The notion of positive conflict suggests also that an outcome of our conflicts may entail facing—without disgrace or disgracing—that some things may not be reconcilable in mutually satisfactory ways, and that we do not have to accept and agree on everything to move on.

These factors about positive conflict support another concept—that of necessary conflict. Necessary conflict refers to the fact that differences often need to be brought to the surface before positive conflict, as described here, can be achieved. It further suggests that to move forward before, during, or after conflict it is important to develop conflict intelligence and to acknowledge the realities of interpersonal disputes and their dynamics. Necessary conflict entails identifying and accepting the difficulties of exchanging hard truths, and the impact of experiencing and expressing strong feelings about relationships and matters that are important to us. It is about learning how to *be*—and participate with an open heart and mind at these times.

Necessary conflict is distinguished from unnecessary conflict, which occurs when one or both disputants engage in impulsive and destructive interactions that escalate to blaming and shaming. By contrast, these dynamics end up firmly packed in the baggage carried from dispute to dispute. Unnecessary conflict lacks positive intent, humility, empathy, and dignity, and the motivation, desire, and ability to choose ways of being and interacting that make conflict an opportunity for growth and learning.

A Few Things I Have Learned About People in Conflict

Over the years in my efforts to help people engage more effectively in conflict, I have learned a lot, including that I have a lot yet to learn. I have learned, for instance, that developing conflict intelligence and mastery is a continuous journey and requires energy, commitment, and the desire to focus on doing so.

It is an understatement to add that I have been constantly reminded along the way that there are many subjective and contextual layers to conflict, and the depth and breadth of relational dynamics affect the emotional, behavioral, cultural, relational, spiritual, and physical elements of our beings. It is mostly as a conflict management coach that I learned about how these dimensions affect us to a degree I had not fully realized in my previous work.

What follows—in no particular order—are some of my other major learnings and reminders gained from my coaching clients' and others' experiences of interpersonal conflict on their way to being and becoming conflict intelligent and masterful. Numerous of these points have been framed as applying to "many of us," as I found them to be especially common. These points and others that are perhaps less common are reflected in the various topics and questions in this book.

- Many of us are off-balance during conflict and even as we prepare to face a potentially challenging situation. This emotional state typically leads to varying degrees of stress, anxiety, lack of concentration, physical symptoms, and a loss of words to express ourselves and what we want or need. At these times, we are also inclined to misinterpret words and body language, and get caught up in a spiral that is fuelled by the negative energy that often accompanies conflict.

- Many of us experience emotional pain when we are in conflict—for example, feelings of rejection, vulnerability, hurt, sadness, negativity, self-loathing, insecurity, guilt, depression, resentment, disappointment, grief, despair, and anger. Our ability to regulate our emotions is often at a low point at these times, and they have the potential for derailing effective connections and communications.

- When emotions grow during conflicts, our problem-solving and decision-making skills deteriorate. With lessened capacity to think things out, our emotions seem to drive our actions and energy. We may then perpetuate a cycle propelled by assumptions, misinterpretations, and other counter-productive reactions. This can be immobilizing, and may also blow matters out of proportion.

- One of the frequent reactions in an interpersonal conflict is to become defensive about something the other person says to us. At these times, we experience—at some level of consciousness—that something meaningful to or about us is being undermined, thwarted, or threatened. We then defend what we perceive is being challenged. This may be a value, need, aspect of our identity,[8] or something else that is important to us. Though it may not necessarily be the intent of the speaker to challenge us in such fundamental ways, we often perceive it is their motive and attribute blame accordingly.

- Though we do not necessarily use the word "shame" to describe one of the experiences of being in conflict, many of us are embarrassed or ashamed about what we said or did, or didn't say or do, during the course of an interpersonal dispute. We may also experience shame when the other person faults us for things we said or did that they perceive as mean, egregious, offensive, and so on. We may hear from her or him a truth we do not want to admit.

- This sense of shame may arise, too, from the reaction of others with whom we discuss our conflicts. Further, for some of us there is shame in seeking help, such as reporting someone's behavior or participating in processes such as coaching, mediation, or counseling because we are unable to sort out our dispute ourselves. At these times, some of us worry about how we are regarded by whomever assists us—possibly resulting in self-criticism and other self-limiting responses as part of feeling shame.

- When self-limiting beliefs go into high gear in conflict, self-talk may sound like, "I shouldn't have said anything"; "I really don't know how to express myself well enough"; and "I was wrong to think I could make a difference." Inner reactions that are full of self-blame, such as these examples, get in the way of confidence and clear thinking. When this happens, we lose the ability to put things into a perspective that does not diminish our view of ourselves. This may result in taking responsibility that is not ours to take. We may compromise or yield to the other person's wishes, to our detriment.

- Certain circumstances bring out the dark side in many of us when we are in conflict. We may then demonstrate conduct that is uncharacteristic, such as treating others poorly and acting in mean-spirited, thoughtless, and hurtful ways.

- Even if we do not directly vocalize what we are thinking and feeling about a conflict situation or the other person who offends us, our bodies, faces, and actions commonly reflect our thoughts and emotions. We are not always aware of the negative power and adverse impact of our demeanor on others.

- A common fear in conflict is the possibility of loss. We may fear losing the relationship, affection, control, and what we are fighting for. Or, we may fear showing weakness and vulnerability. Fears such as these and others lead to a reluctance to initiate a potentially contentious discussion, or to respond to the other person when she or he says or does something that we perceive as an offence.[9] As a result, we may tend to avoid conflict, or we accommodate the other person's needs, or do not stand up for ourselves.

- Being in conflict takes courage. It takes courage to listen to another person's pain directed at us. It requires courage to admit responsibility for our part of the discord. It takes courage to express what we need and believe, and face the possible consequences of the other person's negative pushback and reactions. It takes courage—and dignity and humility—to know when to stand up and when to stand down. It takes courage to acknowledge and accept different perspectives. It takes courage to let go of our expectations and hopes we have about the relationship and the outcome of our disputes. It takes courage to give the other person the benefit of the doubt, to apologize, to forgive, to move on.[10] It takes courage to work on becoming conflict intelligent and masterful, and to live the intention of positive conflict.

- It is often the case that we rewrite in our head and heart what occurred in the conflict for all sorts of reasons, such as to alleviate guilt, to feel better, to justify our contribution, to feel vindicated, and so on. As a consequence, when we re-tell our conflict stories we often distort some or all of the truth.

- Many of us agonize after a conflict and show signs of ongoing stress, unsettled feelings, and self-recrimination. We may hold onto residual hurt, shame, and other emotions—at times for protracted periods. We wish we had said something else, or said it differently, or said nothing at all. The remnants of unmet expectations, unresolved emotions, and unspoken words show up in how we cope and interact in the aftermath of the dispute with the other person, and even with others. We may shroud the next conflict—and the next and the next—with those same remnants.

How This Book Is Designed

Following this introductory chapter, the book is divided into three more chapters titled Before Conflict, During Conflict, and After Conflict. The beginning of each chapter features some preliminary thoughts and considerations about interpersonal conflict relevant to the pertinent timeframe. This is followed by 25 common aspects of conflict relating to the chapter's title. Each topic begins with a description about the specific aspect to be discussed and 12 reflective questions that invite readers to explore the particular area in more detail. The topic and question pages may be reproduced to enhance your use of the workbook.

Some questions are asked in two or more parts. The last two questions of each series are the same throughout. They are, "What else occurs to you as you consider these questions?" and "What insights do you have?" You may also consider, "What questions have yet to be asked?" or, "What answers do you not yet have?" Or, referring to what David Whyte says in his poem "Sometimes," reprinted at the beginning of this book, you may find some "questions that have no right to go away."[11]

There are no right or wrong answers to the questions posed in this book. They are designed to invite readers to consider different ways of looking at and being in conflict.

Metaphors, plays on words, and idioms are used to describe some topics and ask the related questions. I have found that these various methods serve to inspire different ways of thinking and feeling about conflict, ourselves, and the persons with whom we are in dispute. Readers will find some topics and questions resonate more than others, and you may be surprised to find that "when you change the way you look at things, the things you look at change."[12]

The table of contents at the beginning of each chapter lists the topics and page numbers so that you may focus on the particular aspects of conflict you want to explore—which will typically vary from person to person and from situation to situation. In this regard, as you will see throughout, I suggest bringing specific scenarios to mind when answering the questions about the areas you want to examine.

Sometimes a topic may not be pertinent to you, but relates more to what you think the other person is experiencing or doing regarding your interpersonal dispute. Even so, the questions on that subject may serve to shed some light on the dynamic between you and be worth exploring—with just a change of the subjective noun.

Please note that some topics may be more relevant for you in another sequence of time than where it is placed. For instance, the topic **Understanding Why We Blame** is in Chapter 4: After Conflict. Instead, you may be conscious of blaming the other person before or during the conflict. Whenever it is appropriate to do so, then, simply change the verb's tense within the questions on the topics regarding the aspect of a dispute you are exploring.

Please also note that some subjects overlap and are variations on a theme. The language of the title, the content, and the questions are purposely framed in different ways to provide a range of possible approaches with which to explore the topic. Cross-references to related topics are set in bold type.

Reading Audience

The questions in this book may be used by anyone striving to engage in conflict more effectively. You may find this book of particular interest if you like the approach of using reflective questions as a way to explore specific areas of conflict management that you want to develop further. You may find it helpful that the concepts are broken down—in the timeframes of before, during, and after conflict. You may like the idea of shifting the lens with which you view your conflicts and seeing how metaphors, idioms, and different ways of looking at things expand your understanding of the conflict, yourself, and the other person.

The book is also designed to provide tools for those who work in any capacity with people in conflict. You may be a coach, mediator, leader, lawyer, human resource professional, union representative, teacher, psychologist, therapist, social worker, or other practitioner helping clients work through a dispute, and wanting to be more conflict intelligent and masterful. You may be looking for another technique to help people find their way through conflict and improve their proficiency in certain areas. You may find the focus on specific aspects of interpersonal conflict within the before, during, and after timeframes to be beneficial. Finally, you may value reflective questions because their use is compatible with your belief in self-determination and building self-awareness as a major step for making changes in our lives.

CHAPTER TWO

Before Conflict

Before Conflict—Some Preliminary Thoughts to Consider

An interpersonal dispute is often evident not just after it percolates, but while it is brewing. At these times, our increasing awareness about things that provoke us about another person's actions, words, manner, or attitude begin to take hold. The reasons they irritate us are not necessarily clear at these times. However, we still experience some form of inner conflict. That is, at some level of consciousness, we process thoughts and emotions about the other person and the things that are arousing a negative reaction in us. This internal conflict has the potential for erupting in a nanosecond, or it may linger indefinitely. Or, our feelings may surface intermittently in a variety of ways that alert us to ongoing and unsettling discord.

The fact is, it is not unusual to feel we are in conflict even when the other person has no inkling of what we are experiencing. While we are not directly conveying our viewpoints or disgruntled feelings, the inner disharmony is usually more overt than we think, and may be observed and sensed by the other person and those around us. This occurs not only through our body and facial language, but also by the aura we transmit.

Inner conflict is insidious and has a way of creeping slowly into our consciousness. Perhaps we are aware of our growing irritation about things another person says or does, or is not saying or doing. We may have been provoked about these things for a long time, and find ourselves becoming more and more annoyed and on edge around her or him. We may outwardly or inwardly cringe when we observe the particular actions, attitudes, and words that bother us. We may have begun to conduct ourselves in uncharacteristic ways around her or him—being curt, sarcastic, hostile, disdainful, and abrasive. We may have started to ignore this person, act aloof, or walk away when we see her or him near us.

Whether these sorts of responses emanate from us about another person or from someone else about us, they not only provide a sign that something is amiss between us; they actually signal, too, that we have a choice about how to proceed and manage ourselves and the situation before things unnecessarily escalate.

Conflict mastery, as discussed in Chapter 1, is not just about engaging effectively in a conflict once it has evolved. When we become masterful at conflict we are proactive and tap into our feelings and thoughts early on. We consider the reality of what we are sensing. We use our learned and innate abilities to reflect on what is going on for us and with the other person as soon as we sense discord. We consider whether to address the perceived dissension at this point. We assess whether the conflict is likely to evolve if we do not share what we are experiencing.

When we achieve conflict intelligence and mastery, we also contemplate how best to prepare for the possibility or inevitability of things materializing. We think out the optimal approach for initiating a discussion—to discuss what we perceive, gain clarity, and check out our assumptions. And we think out ways of responding in conflict-masterful ways in the event the other person raises related concerns with us.

There are many reasons we may be reluctant to bring up issues early on about things that offend us and stir up negative feelings. Certainly, some situations are best left alone. Others are not. Though we do not always know the optimal tact when we experience inner conflict, we know we do not feel good about a situation, the other person's actions, views, words, and so on, and our own reactions. These are pivotal clues that provide us with the opportunity to think out the conflict dynamic and consider the best way forward.

The thing is, generally speaking, it is not an easy task for many of us to address brewing conflict in its early stages (at least until we have gained conflict mastery). Rather, it is more often a time we tend to wait, hoping the disturbing behavior will stop, improve, or not continue to bother us. Or, we may expect our demeanor will alert the other person to cease the words or conduct we find noxious. Or, we make an off-hand remark, anticipating that she or he will get our indirect message to do so. We may hope, too, that our ongoing negative feelings will subside and not adversely affect the relationship.

During the sorts of machinations just described, we may engage in some self-blame and even some wishful thinking. We may misplace or displace what we are feeling onto unrelated matters or other people. If we do nothing, we may experience a cloud hovering over our personal or professional lives. Doing nothing about what is perturbing us often results, too, in unnecessary conflict surfacing somewhere along the way, propelled by a build-up of disconcerting emotions and assumptions.

This chapter is about the occasions we internally acknowledge that something is going on within us, and between us and another person, that is adversely affecting us. We sense it may evolve and become a challenge for our relationship, and affect something important to us. The topics that follow here therefore invite readers to be alert to those moments when unproductive thoughts, emotions, and assumptions begin to enter our consciousness—before they become externalized.

As conflict intelligence develops, it will be increasingly apparent how these sorts of indicators are gifts. They present us with the chance early on to gain an understanding of the dynamic that is leading to inner discomfort and tension—to take stock of what is going on for us and what we are experiencing in relation to the other person. They urge us to gain perspective and consider the other person's, too. They provide us with the opportunity to be proactive. They signal this is a time to decide how to facilitate a positive conflict experience. They also help define the conflict-mastery skills required to preempt the unnecessary escalation of conflict.

As you begin to explore in this chapter a range of circumstances, emotions, and tendencies that arise before conflict, it helps—as suggested in Chapter 1—to bring to mind specific real-life situations when answering the questions. Doing so provides a context that will increase your insights and learning.

Our Conflict Habits

As you read in Chapter 1, one of the ten premises of this book is that we have the ability to learn new conflict habits. Habits we rely on when it comes to interpersonal conflicts are like other habits that become rote—that we repeat without much thought. In addition to learning them from our families of origin, and our teachers, religious leaders, cultures, peers, bosses, and others, we often learn conflict habits from our various attempts to manage situations based on a range of experiences and observations over time. Some of us also take related courses, or read about recommended techniques that we try to incorporate. Or, we act on someone's advice. Mostly, though, repeated attempts to discover what works and what does not guide our conflict journeys, and we tend to develop and rely on some methods more than others. These are the ones that seem to form our conflict habits.

In whatever ways they have become part of our being, conflict habits reflect the idiosyncratic ways each of us has learned to cope with the sorts of scenarios that adversely affect us and our relationships. And they show up in how we interact and communicate, how we defend things that are important to us, and how we otherwise approach internal and interpersonal conflict. It is an understatement to say some habits work for us better than others.

Whether or not they serve us well, we may not recognize that our particular ways of addressing conflict are habits we can shift. They somehow feel a part of who we are, and so we may resist trying to change them or the notion that we are able to do so. Whether and how to find different ways of engaging in conflict are not possibilities about which many of us give much thought. At least not until, for any number of reasons, we realize our relationships and our well-being are struggling as a consequence of our conflict management style. We may have become increasingly aware of which habits are unproductive or unhealthy. Or, we may experience pressure placed on us in this regard by life or business partners, family members, friends, bosses, peers, and others.

As with other habits, we have the ability to change them, and in the case of conflict engagement, to develop new ways of interacting that reflect how we prefer to be and respond when we encounter discord. And though it takes time, energy, focus, and motivation, the journey to conflict mastery starts with willingness to change.

If you are willing to change one or more of your conflict habits, the first step suggested here is to identify one habit you know is counterproductive, and answer the following questions about it. The same questions may be repeated for other habits you wish to improve.

QUESTIONS

- How do you describe one of your conflict habits you want to change, that is, how is it manifested?

- What might caring friends or family who know you, and have observed you demonstrate this habit, add to your description (your response to the previous question), if anything? What, if anything, might they say differently?

- What is the impact that using this habit has on you? How do others experience it, that is, those on the receiving end?

- What appears to be the impact on caring others who have observed you using this habit? What might they suggest as alternative ways to be and interact?

- How do you think you developed this habit? Under what circumstances have you *not* used it? What accounts for the difference?

- How do you prefer to be, and be seen, regarding this habit?

- How do you expect your conflict interactions will be different when you interact in the manner you prefer (as you described in the previous question)?

- How, specifically, do you want people with whom you have conflict to experience your preferred way of interacting? What would you most like your caring others to compliment you on when you interact in the way you prefer?

- How much do you want to change this habit on a scale of 1 to 5, 5 being "very much"? If you scored 4 or lower, what reservations do you have about changing this habit?

- How may you be getting in your own way from beginning to change the habit? How might you overcome that? What is one step to take immediately to make a positive change regarding this habit?

- What else occurs to you as you consider these questions?

- What insights do you have?

Hot Buttons

Hot buttons, also called trigger points, may be generally defined as actions, words, and attitudes of others that evoke a negative reaction in us—inner, external, or both. It may be what someone says or does, or does not say or do. It may be a mood, a way of acting, or facial and body language that triggers us.

We are not usually aware, at least consciously, of what other people's hot buttons are. Exceptions are likely those of our life partners, family, friends, and colleagues and co-workers whom we come to know well. New relationships start with a clean slate. In any case, it is common that we discover another's trigger points, and they ours, the hard way. That is, generally speaking, we do not know what offends or irritates us or others—including the effects—until hot buttons are pushed.

Depending on numerous factors, there are various ways we react to the experience of others pushing our hot buttons. The first time someone pushes one, we may choose not to get upset about what is provoking us. It may take repeated times until our discomfort grows and we say anything—if we decide to say anything at all.

Whether we react early on or after several incidents, some of us let the person know directly that she or he is irritating us, and sometimes with strong emotions that fuel a conflict. Others of us are more covert or indirect—showing signs of being disgruntled without really saying what is happening. Our reactions may be so indirect that they are missed altogether.

Not all situations in which we or others are triggered necessarily lead to conflict. However, once our tempers rise and we "lose our cool," we are usually unable to effectively contemplate and identify what specifically contributed to the escalation in the first place.

In the quest for conflict mastery, whenever it is evident that something is creating internal discord for us, it helps to take some time to step back, remain curious about the specific irritant, and consider why it bothers us. As discussed in Chapter 1 and in this chapter, determining what we ourselves are saying or doing that may be contributing to the dynamic is also part of a conflict analysis. Such an examination is paramount in our efforts to become increasingly proficient in engaging in conflict.

Here are some pertinent questions that aim to heighten awareness about your hot buttons, including what it may take to cool it down. Some questions ask you to consider the other person's hot buttons in the same situation, too.

QUESTIONS

- In one interaction between you and the other person, what, specifically, did she or he say or do that pushed your hot button? Or, what did she or he not say or do? Or, how did she or he act that triggered you?

- If you identified more than one trigger point here, select one to start with. What makes that a hot button for you? What value or values did you perceive being undermined, if any, when the person pushed your hot button? What did you need from her or him? What aspect or aspects of your identity, if any, may have felt challenged?

- For what reasons do you think the other person pushed your hot button? What other reasons might she or he give that are different from what you are thinking?

- What do you think you were letting the other person do that is actually within your control?

- If the other person reacted to something you said or did (or did not say or do, or the way you acted) in the same scenario, what reaction did you see or hear? To what specifically was she or he reacting, from what you could tell?

- What might make that a hot button for the other person—such as what value might she or he have perceived as being undermined? What aspect of her or his identity might have felt challenged? What did the other person need from you?

- What reason or reasons motivated you to say or do whatever triggered the other person? From what you can tell, how might she or he have interpreted your reason or reasons that may be different from what you intended?

- What are three conflict-masterful ways to respond when someone pushes your buttons? What are three conflict-masterful ways to prevent pushing someone else's buttons?

- What are you learning about possible ways to cool your hot buttons in your conflict interactions? What else do you want to learn on this topic?

- What has occurred to you about hot buttons now that did not occur to you when you started this series of questions?

- What else occurs to you as you consider these questions?

- What insights do you have?

Picking Up the Conflict Vibes

Before conflict emerges we often pick up "vibrations," or "vibes," that signal dissension within ourselves or in what we sense coming from another person. Picking up such vibes provides a prompt for us to step back and contemplate what is occurring. They alert us to pay attention to our observations and instincts to explore what seems to be igniting us, or the other person, or both. Similarly, the vibes urge us to check out what we are sensing to be able to gain clarity and focus—qualities that have the potential for getting lost when we begin to experience unsettling feelings.

Essentially, then, vibes reflect our sense that there is disharmony when the signals and other signs described above appear. And whether we pick up someone else's or we are putting out vibrations ourselves, it is evident that things are amiss and adversely affecting our interactions.

Often, we pick up vibes and react, at least internally, when we perceive that the other person is relating to us differently. Clues may be that she or he appears distant, does not engage us in conversation, makes off-hand or sarcastic remarks, or looks away or avoids us when we try to connect. We pick up subtle and not so subtle signs, too, from the other person's body and facial language that convey her or his negative feelings toward us.

Paying attention to conflict vibes when they arise not only provides an opportunity to consider what is occurring. The experience also gives us a chance to choose whether it is prudent to address the dynamic at this time—and if so, how to proceed. Such a proactive approach helps us to prevent unnecessary conflict from escalating (a concept discussed in Chapter 1). It prepares us, too, for the possibility of necessary conflict, including constructive ways to bring matters that need to be aired to the surface for discussion.

The following self-reflective questions concentrate on what is occurring within a situation in which you are picking up vibes. Also, some questions focus on a situation in which you are putting out conflict vibes. It could be the same situation or another. The next topic in this chapter, **Acting on Simmering Signs**, develops these concepts in a different way.

QUESTIONS

- To start with, how do you describe the vibes you sense that the other person is putting out, that is, her or his actions, attitude, and so on?

- How are you experiencing the vibes?

- What does your intuition tell you about the reason(s) the other person is putting out these vibes (your answer to the first question)? Why that reason or those reasons?

- What do you trust about your instincts here? What do you not trust about your instincts, if that is the case?

- In what ways may you have contributed to the other person's putting out vibes toward you (things you might not have already considered in your previous answers)?

- What is keeping you from checking out—with the other person—the vibes you are experiencing? What conflict-masterful approach might work if you decide to do this? If you prefer not to, why is that so?

- How do you describe the sorts of vibes you are putting out in this interaction (or another interaction, if you do not think you are doing so in this one)? How might the other person describe your vibes in the conflict you have in mind? How might she or he be experiencing them?

- For what reasons are you putting out those vibes? What, specifically, do you think you are conveying through your actions, words, demeanor, and so on that the other person is likely picking up?

- What is keeping you from more directly expressing to the other person what is bothering you? What might be keeping the other person from asking you?

- What would you like to have happen between you and the other person in the interaction in which you are putting out vibes? What might you say or do to achieve that outcome?

- What else occurs to you as you consider these questions?

- What insights do you have?

Acting on Simmering Signs

Starting as children and over the years of interacting in a wide range of contexts, we learn and develop views about what constitutes acceptable and unacceptable actions, words, attitudes, styles of communicating, ways of treating others, and so on. We aim to demonstrate the behaviors we consider appropriate, and we generally expect others to share our ideas of what appropriate is. However, there are times when our actions do not align with our values or those of others with whom we interact. Similarly, there are times people act in ways that are not compatible with their values or ours.

When we are on the receiving end of someone's behaviors that do not fit with our beliefs about what is acceptable, many of us tend to make judgments about the person and her or his character and motives. We may also have developed stereotypes and biases that we apply at these times. The thing is—though some behaviors are inexcusable—in many of our day-to-day interactions we do not always understand that our rulebooks on what constitutes acceptable behavior and communication are different from others' rulebooks. Or, that the meaning we give another person's deeds and words does not accurately reflect her or his intent.

Simmering signs that things are amiss between oneself and another person are detected as soon as we sense some internal upset and begin to judge the other person—or even ourselves. Signs may include physical reactions such as a churning stomach, increased heart rate, red face, fidgeting, and so on. Or, they may be general negative thoughts and feelings, or specifically ones about the other person. In any case, the reasons for whatever we are experiencing are not always easily identifiable. As with **Picking Up the Conflict Vibes**, the previous topic, this is an opportune time—when we start to feel things simmering inside us—to probe our thinking and emotions to be able to gain an understanding of what seems to be happening.

Your answers to the following questions will yield some other ways of viewing yourself, the situation, and the other person when simmering signs appear.

QUESTIONS

- Try to imagine a scenario or person about which you are sensing at least one simmering sign that things are amiss. What specifically seems to be simmering that is arousing that inner reaction in you?

- How do you describe your inner reaction? In what way(s) might the other person notice that?

- What do you think initiated the simmering? If you do not know, what possibilities occur to you? Or, what possibilities might someone observing the dynamics between you suggest?

- What could boil over that worries you most? If things continue to simmer to the point of boiling over, what would you look back at and wish you had said or done?

- If what worries you does happen, what positive outcome might you want to strive for?

- How will you respond and make that outcome happen in a conflict-masterful way if what concerns you does occur? What will your conflict-masterful approach be like in more detail?

- How is that response and approach different from what you usually do at such times?

- What do you imagine it will feel like to take this different approach? How do you hope it will be for the other person?

- What challenges do you want to be prepared for? How will you handle those?

- Now that you are thinking this matter through, what opportunities have the simmering signs provided for you and the other person?

- What else occurs to you as you consider these questions?

- What insights do you have?

Thinking About Whether to Raise the Issue

Many of us grapple with when or whether to raise a potentially contentious issue with another. The opportunity to make this determination commonly presents itself when we notice some internal or external sense of unrest about an interaction, such as those described in **Picking Up the Conflict Vibes** and **Acting on Simmering Signs**. Sometimes when our gut instincts alert us that something is off, we may question them and wonder, "Is it really worth it to bring up this matter?," or "Am I making a big deal out of nothing?," and other such self-inquiry. Uncertainties of all sorts contribute to tentativeness, and we face indecision about whether to attend to what we sense or leave it alone.

Deciding what makes a seemingly or potentially conflictual matter worth raising is a tough call—especially when emotions begin to prevail. However, under most circumstances, exploring what the issue or issues mean to us and the benefits and disadvantages of addressing them is a good starting point. Doing so usually gives us a better understanding of what we are experiencing regarding any fears, ambivalences, worries, and our motivations, expectations, and hopes. Possible challenges to the relationship and our well-being are also considerations in an analysis of this nature.

Reflective queries about whether to raise an issue that may be contentious, then, not only help us to clarify the advantages and disadvantages of initiating a discussion about what we perceive is happening. They also invite an exploration of whether we are prepared to face the potential risks that may emerge as part of our analysis.

There may be occasions, of course, when we decide that it is not prudent, smart, or appropriate to raise a matter. But if we are reluctant because we tend to avoid conflict or are experiencing fears or other emotions that impede us, it is important to contemplate how such factors negatively contribute to the dynamic and the way forward.

The next series of questions provide another approach when thinking about whether to raise with another person a specific conflict issue. (The word "issue" is singularized in these questions. If there are a number of matters you are considering raising, it helps to explore one at a time, as the responses often vary from one issue to another.)

QUESTIONS

- What is the issue you are thinking about raising? What makes it contentious?

- What are the risks of raising the issue for you? What are the risks of your raising the issue for the other person? What else worries you about bringing it up?

- What are the opportunities for you if you raise the issue? What are the opportunities for the other person?

- If you decide not to raise the issue, what then?

- How would you like things to be between you and the other person, instead of what is currently happening because of the conflict between you?

- How important is the relationship to you on a scale of 1 to 5, 5 being "extremely important" and 1 being "not at all"? How important is the issue in dispute on the same scale?

- If the relationship is more important to you than the issue (or even if you've given them the same rating), what do you need or want from the other person so as not to let the conflict damage your relationship? What may she or he need from you?

- If the issue is more important to you than the relationship (or even if you've given them the same rating), what are the options for settling it? What are the advantages and disadvantages of those options for you? For the other person?

- When you have raised issues with others in the past and had a successful outcome, what have you done well in your communications? What has not worked well that you will not repeat?

- What are you thinking now about whether to raise the issue?

- What else occurs to you as you consider these questions?

- What insights do you have?

The Platinum Moment of Choice in Conflict

As just discussed, it is common that at times we are reticent to initiate a dialogue about things that have the potential for leading to conflict, or escalating existing discord. Apprehensions may include possible retaliation, encountering some sort of confrontational reaction, becoming more upset, chancing a threat to the relationship, or the fear that nothing positive will come from raising the matter or matters.

We may know that suppressing our feelings as a consequence of not dealing with interpersonal conflict has an adverse impact on our physical and emotional health. We may realize, too, from experience, that unresolved thoughts and feelings often erupt somewhere else. For instance, they may continually emerge in repeated negative interactions with the same person or others, and can be just as, or even more, unsettling.

The fact is, we have choices about how to manage ourselves and our reactions when conflict presents itself, and considering what they are at these times is an indicator of conflict intelligence. Other indicators include being clear on what we intend to accomplish if we proceed, contemplating what is important to us and the other person, determining the optimal timing, and preparing effective ways to communicate.

What this means, essentially, is that we have a choice as to when and how we initiate a conversation about perceived dissension—with the goal of short-circuiting unnecessary conflict. These moments are referred to here as "platinum moments of choice," and there are many possibilities. For instance, we have a choice about how to facilitate a thoughtful and conciliatory discussion about what is happening. We have a choice not to demonize the person or ourselves. We have choices about how we want to be in our conflict interactions. And we have a choice, upon reflection, to decide that it is not appropriate for us to say or do anything. (In Chapter 3, this aspect is explored in the topic **Choices About Responding When in Conflict**.)

The following questions invite you to consider the ideal moments that arise for exploring signs of conflict before you and the other person become involved in an unnecessary negative dynamic.

QUESTIONS

- Based on the concept of platinum moment of choice as described above, how else might you describe what this expression means—as you interpret it?

- Try to imagine an interaction about which you are currently experiencing tension. What was your first internal indication that discord exists—emotionally, cognitively, or in your body?

- What makes that indication (your answer to the previous question) especially disconcerting for you? To what, specifically, do you attribute that reaction?

- What might have made that a platinum moment for letting the other person know that you are reacting to something she or he said or did—or did not say or do?

- In what ways might it have also been a platinum moment of choice for the other person, if you had raised it with her or him at that time?

- How might that *not* have been a platinum moment of choice for you? In what ways may it not have been platinum for her or him?

- At what other point or points within the relationship or before the interaction—or even since—may there have been platinum moments of choice to do or say something regarding your sense of the tension between you? What could you have said or done at one or more of these points? What makes each of those points platinum?

- What specifically stopped you from saying something?

- Now that you have thought about this, what, in your view, makes something a platinum moment of choice that you had not considered before?

- In the future, how will you choose your platinum moments of choice before acting or reacting?

- What else occurs to you as you consider these questions?

- What insights do you have?

Picking Fights

Sometimes we get into a cranky mood for no apparent reason. We may be bored, feeling unwell, or lacking energy, or we may be generally unhappy with work, events occurring in our lives, or one or more relationships. We may be out of sorts because we have onerous things on our minds, or people are pressuring us about a myriad of matters. Personal and professional obligations also cause us stress and weigh us down. Or, we do not set boundaries. Or, we feel hurt by a lingering or current situation in which someone's actions or words upset us.

As we know, these and other types of happenings in our everyday lives contribute to a state of mind and heart that negatively affects us and those around us. Such dynamics often form at least some of the variables that ultimately lead to conflict. Common responses when conflict emerges are to flee, to fight, or to freeze. This topic is about a tendency to fight, and for some of us, this may be a habit.

In situations that affect our sense of well-being, especially when we feel bogged down by life's travails, we may be more reactive, vulnerable, and overly sensitive to others' comments and actions. We may judge and find fault easily. We may act in ways in which we are untrue to ourselves. We may project or impose our views, and take strong and even unreasonable stands on issues. We may take out our emotions on someone who becomes the target of our state of mind and heart, and pick fights.

Picking a fight is a deliberate act, and this point resonates with the notion of platinum moment of choice, just discussed. That is, we are able to choose not to fight. This is an important message to tell ourselves when we are becoming defensive and beginning to react in ways that are counterproductive—and which in other circumstances result in picking a fight.

The following line of inquiry helps to examine in more detail what is happening for you when you find yourself about to pick a fight, and what options may exist. (More on this conflict area is discussed in Chapter 3 under the topic **Fighting When in Conflict**.)

QUESTIONS

- Try to imagine a specific situation in which you are tending to pick a fight. What is compelling you to do so? What is happening in your life that may also be contributing to your inclination to pick a fight?

- What may compel the other person to engage in the fight with you, if that is applicable?

- What would be a successful outcome for you if you picked a fight?

- What if you choose to fight and you "win" according to what you were hoping to achieve as a successful outcome—how would that be for you? How might it be for the other person?

- In what ways might things change between you and the other person in a positive way as a result of your picking a fight? How might it change things in not so positive ways?

- What might be an unsuccessful outcome for you in this situation, if you pick a fight—other than what you may already have referred to in the previous question?

- What might picking a fight achieve that other options are not likely to achieve? Why is that the case?

- Besides picking a fight, what other possible choice(s) might work? What might make such a choice or choices workable? How might such a choice or choices be workable for the other person, too?

- What else do you need to know or learn that will influence your choice of whether or not to pick a fight? What are the conflict-masterful options when it comes to what you might do other than pick a fight?

- In what ways does the idea of picking a fight become stronger in answering the questions here? Why is that so? How has the idea of picking a fight decreased in strength? Why is that so?

- What else occurs to you as you consider these questions?

- What insights do you have?

Freezing

What does freezing mean in the context of conflict? Freezing is one reaction to being provoked during a conflict—fighting and fleeing are two other common responses. It has been suggested that freezing is different from "being stuck" (see the topic **Getting Unstuck When in Conflict** in Chapter 3). This suggestion is based on the notion that being stuck is a more transient state of being during conflict, whereas freezing, as it is described here, is more like being unable to engage at all when provoked. That is, freezing is immobilizing.

Freezing may be a reaction to conflict that reflects helplessness and powerlessness to know what to say or do. It may be a fear response, a shutdown of our usual skills and ability to process information and emotions, or both. It may be a matter of becoming cold internally or toward the other person (or both) as a way to stave off tension and the depth of our emotions.

These and other ways in which freezing affects us have a huge impact on the course our interpersonal conflicts take and the outcomes. In an effort to thaw out a freeze response, it helps to deconstruct what is happening at the times when we freeze or the other person does so. The following questions facilitate such a process.

QUESTIONS

- Try to imagine a conflict when you froze. How would you describe what freezing was like?

- What specifically felt "frozen" for you?

- What impact did your freezing have on the other person? How did freezing affect the specific conflict interaction?

- With what would you want to replace freezing in the context of this conflict? What would be different about the interaction if that occurred?

- If you do not want to thaw out, why is that so?

- How do you describe what you have observed when the other person in a conflict with you freezes? What is the impact on you at these times?

- How do you suppose you might help the other person in a conflict interaction to thaw out, if you want or wanted to? What difference might that make?

- Generally, what positive outcomes come from freezing? What not so positive ones?

- Generally, when you have reacted to being provoked in other conflict inter-actions—without freezing—what was different in that situation or those situations? What did you do differently? What different outcomes resulted?

- What learning might you apply from your previous experiences (your answer to the question above) in the future? What else do you think it would take for you to thaw out, if you wanted to, when you freeze in response to a conflict?

- What else occurs to you as you consider these questions?

- What insights do you have?

Avoiding Interpersonal Conflict

Our ways of engaging in conflict depend on many factors, and we choose a variety of methods—consciously or not—that help us find our way through it. Some variables influencing how we react and interact include our relationship with the other person, our history with them, the timing, and our mood at the time. Determinants also include the degree of offense we are experiencing, what is at stake if we avoid or do not avoid the situation, the emotional impact of the dispute on each of us and others, and what we are feeling in the moment about our lives.

Many of us have a conflict management style that has not worked well for us but becomes our default approach when we are under stress. That is, even when we learn constructive ways of being in conflict, we may at times rely on time-worn habits that have proven—from past experiences—to serve us poorly. It seems that overcoming the common tendency to *avoid* can be a challenge for many of us.

Avoiding conflict is somewhat akin to fleeing—one of the three common responses to provocation. Like fighting and freezing, avoiding or fleeing is one choice we have when faced with conflict, and sometimes it works as the optimal approach. Other times, we avoid conflict to our detriment. There are possible advantages and disadvantages in all decisions we make about whether to step up to dissension we are experiencing. The thing is, one of the results of avoiding conflict is that it leads to *a void* that is often filled with continuing feelings of confusion and upset.

We may know intellectually that the potential for resolving the issues, gaining a better understanding of what is happening, reconciling the relationship, and improving communications exists if we face the conflict. The unknown and lack of certainty, however, often create unsettling feelings, and we choose avoidance. For instance, we may fear the relationship will suffer, that we will lose control, or that our hopes and needs will not be met. We may worry, too, about a range of other possible repercussions, such as harsh words, hostility, ongoing negativity, and alienation, and that emotions will take over such that nothing will be reconciled. We may avoid also because we are overwhelmed and just want to get away from the tension.

In the end, it takes courage to learn and use effective ways to engage in conflict if we tend to avoid it. And it takes courage to discern when avoidance is the optimal response, and learn and use effective ways to walk away from conflict. That said, a pattern in which the consistent choice is to avoid conflict is not compatible with efforts to learn what it takes to be with the discord in conflict-masterful ways. So, examining when and why we avoid conflict is a helpful exercise in the quest for conflict mastery. Here are some relevant questions about this topic.

QUESTIONS

- Under what circumstances do you usually avoid conflict? Generally speaking, what is it that you are avoiding in these circumstances? With regard to a conflict you are avoiding, what specifically are you avoiding in that one? Why are you doing so?

- What are the advantages for you of avoiding that situation? What are the disadvantages for you? What are the advantages for the other person that you are avoiding this situation? What are the disadvantages for her or him?

- How might the other person interpret your avoidance in a way that you prefer she or he does not?

- If you have not yet answered these questions, what will it be like for you if you continue to avoid the conflict? What is likely to happen with the conflict? What is likely to occur in your relationship with the other person?

- If you experience *a void* when you avoid conflict, how else might you describe the void or other feelings you experience?

- If the concept of fleeing applies to you and the ways in which you avoid conflict, what would you say you are fleeing from? What are you fleeing to?

- When someone else avoids a conflict with you, what do you observe about her or him? What is it like to be on the receiving end of someone's avoiding conflict?

- What do you suppose it would take for you to stop avoiding?

- What approach or approaches to conflict do you want to master that will work more effectively than avoiding?

- If you reconsider the current situation that you are avoiding, in what ways would that approach or approaches work for you (your answer to the previous question)? In what ways would that approach or approaches work for the other person?

- What else occurs to you as you consider these questions?

- What insights do you have?

Bottling Things Up

"Bottling things up" essentially refers to the inclination to keep things inside—to contain our thoughts and feelings with a reluctance to share them. When it comes to conflict, decisions about whether to raise a potentially contentious issue with someone, and how and when to do so, are especially complicated for those who have a tendency to keep things inside. Similarly, if we tend to bottle things up, we may be reluctant to respond when someone else brings up a matter with us.

We may be well aware that discussing issues that are in dispute with a view to resolving them and healing the relationship is a good idea. However, fears that things may get worse, past experiences that have resulted in negative outcomes, time-worn habits, the inclination to avoid or flee from conflict, and other reasons contribute to bottling things up.

To take the imagery of bottling things up a little further, if this phrase describes you and you want to explore this tendency, it helps to begin by picturing the bottle. Depending on the situation and the other person, you may view what is in it as inconsequential. This may mean you see some stuff in the bottle, but not much to fuss about. You may think the stuff smells a bit, but you can live with it.

As thoughts and emotions begin to grow—through repeated and noxious interactions with the other person—picture the bottle becoming fuller. The contents are murky, smelly, and not very appetizing, and the impact is becoming more toxic. When this occurs it is likely evident to the other person, and even to bystanders, that things are building up for you. That is, you may look and feel as though you are on the brink of overflowing—in a not very pleasant way.

This series of questions asks you to consider a situation in which this expression, "bottling things up," applies to you. Your answers will hopefully facilitate the decision about whether to say something about a situation that is bothering you. The questions and your answers may also help you consider conflict-masterful responses to someone else's efforts to raise matters when you are inclined to bottle things up.

QUESTIONS

- If you tend to bottle things up, what does the bottle represent (that is, in what place are you containing your thoughts and feelings)?

- What emotions are you bottling up about the specific situation you have in mind? What percentage of the bottle is consumed with these emotions? What thoughts are you bottling up regarding that same situation? What percentage of the bottle is consumed with your thoughts?

- If you were to draw the bottle showing the part and percentage that represent your emotions and the part and percentage that represent your thoughts, what would that look like?

- Which of your emotions might you pour out at this time because, as you think about it now, they really do not belong in the bottle? What else could you say or do at this point to reduce the build-up of your negative emotions about the situation or the other person?

- What thoughts might you pour out now because, as you think about it, they really do not belong in the bottle? What else could you say or do at this time to reduce the build-up of your unproductive thoughts?

- What else that you have not mentioned yet is contained in the bottle that is unhealthy? What will it take for you to pour those contents out?

- If you prefer to keep things bottled up and contain your thoughts and feelings and anything else inside, why is that so?

- If you ultimately decide to empty the bottle, what will be the last thought, feeling, or other ingredient that you will pour out? What is healthy in there that you will retain?

- What do you think it will feel like to empty the bottle?

- When you begin to bottle things up at a future time, what might you do differently if you don't want to repeat this response?

- What else occurs to you as you consider these questions?

- What insights do you have?

What Is Your Achilles Heel?

The derivation of the expression "Achilles heel"[1] dates back to an ancient legend. The story goes that Achilles' mother, Thetis, dipped him into the river Styx to make him invulnerable. One of his heels was not covered by the water, though, and he was later killed by an arrow wound to the heel that was exposed. The expression "Achilles heel" is still used today as a metaphor for vulnerability and may be compared—to some extent—to **Hot Buttons**, discussed earlier in this chapter.

Our vulnerabilities often become exposed when we are in conflict. Or, they may lead to the initial discord. For example, if another person knows our area of vulnerability and wants to hurt us, she or he may purposely say or do something to wound our Achilles heel. Sometimes, of course, there is no intent, but our Achilles heel may be struck inadvertently, too. In any case, taking time to reflect on what is happening in the interrelational dynamic, and why, helps in the effort to build conflict intelligence.

Here is a series of questions to help you consider your Achilles heel and the area of vulnerability that results in conflict for you. The questions are designed also to help you gain a better understanding about the exposure you experience at these times, and what positive things your sensitive spots may represent. (If you have more than one area you consider your Achilles heel, it is suggested that you answer the questions by considering one area at a time.)

QUESTIONS

- What would you say is your Achilles heel—an area of vulnerability that is likely to result in conflict when touched?

- What makes this your Achilles heel?

- What, specifically, feels wounded when someone touches your Achilles heel? How does it feel?

- In what ways do you expose your Achilles heel, if you are aware of doing so? How do you appear or act when it feels wounded?

- If you try to hide your vulnerable point, how do you do this?

- What do you *not* know about your Achilles heel?

- What helps diminish the impact on you when you sense someone coming close to touching your Achilles heel? How else may you respond when someone touches your Achilles heel that shows you are well able to manage the provocation?

- How might you strengthen your Achilles heel so that you feel less vulnerable? How will you appear differently if you strengthen your Achilles heel?

- What about your Achilles heel actually represents one or more of your strengths? How will you appear differently if you accept that your vulnerability is a strength?

- How may the knowledge that your Achilles heel represents one or more of your strengths (your answers to the previous questions) help you in your quest for conflict mastery?

- What else occurs to you as you consider these questions?

- What insights do you have?

Conflict Jitters

In addition to the other responses to possible conflict discussed so far, when we expect that an interaction is likely to be contentious, the chances are that many of us get the "jitters." This means we may feel anxious, nervous, fidgety, and generally unsettled. We may fret and become preoccupied about what the other person may say or do, how we will cope, whether things will get out of hand, and so on. It is an understatement to say that jitter-causing stimuli get in the way of engaging effectively in conflict. It may be why some people choose to avoid interactions that are potentially discordant, or bottle things up.

Often the reasons for jitters have to do with fears that do not necessarily have a basis in reality. However, previous experiences, others' narratives about what has happened to them in like circumstances, and a wide range of other influences may result in our dreading conflict. The jitters may even contribute to the negative course the conflict takes, because we lose our equilibrium at these times. None of these reactions, of course, facilitates our efforts to become conflict masterful.

To alleviate conflict jitters, it helps to literally and figuratively step back as much as possible before engaging in an interaction about which we feel flustered and anxious. By doing so, we are more likely to figure out what is needed to manage the situation effectively and preempt unnecessary conflict. The following questions encourage the sorts of reflections that may enable you to do so, if this notion of conflict jitters applies to you. (More on the subject of fears is discussed in Chapter 1 and in the topic **Fears About Being in Conflict** in Chapter 3.)

QUESTIONS

- Under what sorts of circumstances do you get the conflict jitters?

- Try to imagine a specific conflict situation that is giving you the jitters. For what reasons are you experiencing them? How would you describe the jitters?

- What fears, if any, are you experiencing regarding this situation, if you have not yet mentioned them?

- If applicable, how realistic are the fears in the situation you have in mind, rating each on a scale of 1 to 5, 5 being "absolutely realistic" and 1 being "not realistic at all"? If you rated 4 or less, what is not absolutely realistic?

- How are the jitters helping you be proactive and effective about the situation? How are the jitters not helping you? What are you forfeiting by having the jitters? If you did not have jitters about this conflict, what would you be saying or doing differently?

- What is within your control regarding this conflict? What are your strengths when it comes to managing conflict that you might use in this situation?

- How else might you look at this situation to help reduce the jitters? For instance, a year from now, what learning do you want to be able to say you gained from it?

- How are you viewing the other person in this situation? How might you look at her or him differently to take back the power you may be handing over?

- Who will you be in this situation without the jitters? How will you be?

- When you reach a place where the jitters will not interfere with how you proceed with this potential conflict or others, what will you say or do differently (or how will you otherwise be different)? With what will you have replaced the jitters?

- What else occurs to you as you consider these questions?

- What insights do you have?

Chip on the Shoulder

According to Wikipedia, the expression that someone has a "chip on the shoulder" has a rich history dating back to 1756 and an incident at the Royal Navy Dockyards. There was apparently a requirement for shipwrights to carry timber chips under their arms, rather than their shoulders, because they could transport more that way. The story goes that one shipwright, John Miller, refused an order to carry timber chips under his arms and the master shipwright tried to physically force Miller to do so. Miller and others pushed the master and first assistant out of the gateway while keeping the chips on their shoulders. Accordingly, the phrase "chip on the shoulder" came to mean an attitude that dares the other person to refute a challenge on a matter.[2]

These days, if we say someone has a chip on her or his shoulder we are using the expression in much the same way, and also to refer to people who appear to be defensive, angry, bitter, and resentful, who bear grudges and act like victims. Such impressions may be interpreted from a person's demeanor, attitude, tone of voice, facial expressions, and body and verbal language.

Seeing and communicating with people who have a chip on their shoulder, as we perceive them, can be an off-putting and challenging experience. The interrelational dynamic that evolves as a consequence may even lead to conflict.

If you find yourself reacting to another person who, in your view, has a chip on her or his shoulder, the following questions may assist your quest for conflict mastery to be able to be proactive and manage this facade. (This topic and the next two—**The Cold Shoulder** and **That Put My Back Up**—all discuss the body language of conflict. Chapter 3 contains several more topics on this aspect of how we manifest emotions, namely, **Body and Facial Language of Conflict** and **Getting Your Nose Out of Joint**. Chapter 4 discusses this area under the topic **Observing Ourselves Through Someone Else's Eyes**.)

QUESTIONS

- Try to imagine a particular situation in which someone appears to have a chip on her or his shoulder toward you. How would you describe what that looks like?

- What impact does the perceived chip on this person's shoulder have on you?

- What do you suppose that chip is made of to have that sort of impact (your response to the previous question)?

- What about the chip on this person's shoulder contributes to the possibility of a conflict evolving between you?

- What, if anything, may you have said (or may be saying) or have done (or may be doing) that is contributing to her or his chip on the shoulder?

- What do you not know about the person who is carrying a chip on her or his shoulder that you would like to know?

- If you have observed a chip on someone else's shoulder that is not directed at you, what do you see—more objectively—that conjures up different responses in you (if it does)? What are those responses?

- For a minute, picture yourself as someone who is carrying a chip on your shoulder. What is that experience like as you imagine it? What do you imagine you need from others at this time (if you are carrying a chip on your shoulder)?

- What do you think there is to learn from people who carry chips on their shoulders?

- Going forward, how might you respond to the person in the particular situation you discussed here—or generally to people who carry chips on their shoulders—in a way that reflects conflict mastery?

- What else occurs to you as you consider these questions?

- What insights do you have?

The Cold Shoulder

One of the many possible reactions to people who provoke us is to give them "the cold shoulder." This is another metaphor referring to the shoulder that provides a visual description of the ways in which emotions during interpersonal conflicts may be conveyed. Like the phrase "chip on the shoulder," a "cold shoulder" conjures up a vivid image that expresses a great deal in a few words about body language that is sometimes demonstrated in conflict situations. The exact origin of this phrase is not definitive, but it is typically used to express an act of dismissing or disregarding someone.

The first occurrence of the phrase "cold shoulder" in print was apparently by Sir Walter Scott in *The Antiquary*.[3] Descriptors include aloofness and disdain. Another explanation is that the term stems from a direct yet subtle way to serve food to an unwanted guest, that is, by serving an inferior cut of meat ("cold shoulder of mutton") as opposed to a hot meal or a roast fresh out of the oven,[4] which was customary hospitality at the time. A third source claims it is a literal action: placing one's back toward, or at least keeping a shoulder between, a person one is trying to avoid.[5]

When it comes to conflict, the physical representation of a cold shoulder, then, may refer to literally turning away from and avoiding the other person in a dismissive or contemptuous way. Or, it may be an obvious lack of warmth and openness demonstrated by minimal, if any, communications.

We know that when we experience negative emotions toward someone, such as when a conflict is brewing, we typically show we are upset in various ways besides what comes out of our mouths. Our facial and body language speak volumes, and we pick up signals of other people's negative feelings, too, when we observe their physical reactions. We may not always correctly identify what we are seeing and sensing. However, many of us are able to interpret somatic messages, such as a cold shoulder, with some degree of accuracy. It does not mean, however, that we know the reasons for such behavior.

For this set of questions, it helps to consider two situations—one in which you are experiencing or have experienced someone giving you the cold shoulder. The other involves giving someone else the cold shoulder, if you have ever done so. As with many behaviors, this one may happen at various stages of conflict, and whenever it occurs it is an opportune time to engage with the other person. If the engagement is initiated as soon as it happens—which is commonly before conflict emerges—the timing is ripe to prevent unnecessary escalation of a dispute.

QUESTIONS

- How would you describe the cold shoulder you are experiencing from another person? What is the coldest part about it?

- What messages are you inferring from the other person's cold shoulder? What is her or his cold shoulder accomplishing? What is it not accomplishing?

- What do you think the person's reasons are for giving you the cold shoulder? What reasons do you know for certain? If you do not know the reasons, what are some possibilities?

- What would it take for you to engage the other person in conversation to be able to find out what is happening? What concerns do you have about doing so, if you feel reluctant?

- To look at this another way, generally speaking, under what circumstances, if any, have you given someone else the cold shoulder, in this or another conflict? What does it feel like?

- If you are or were giving the cold shoulder to another person in a specific situation, how would you describe what you are or were doing? How do you think the other person might describe your cold shoulder? What might it feel like to her or him?

- For what reasons are you choosing, or did you choose, to give the cold shoulder?

- What message(s) are you, or were you, meaning to convey by giving the other person the cold shoulder? What messages do you think the other person is receiving, or received, that align with your intent? What messages might she or he be receiving, or have received, that do not align with your intent?

- What would it take for you to give a "warm shoulder" instead of a cold one in this situation? Generally, what would a warm shoulder look like as compared to a cold shoulder, whether it is you or the other person giving it?

- What is a conflict-masterful response to another person—rather than giving the cold shoulder—when in conflict? How might you respond in conflict-masterful ways to people with whom you are in conflict, who demonstrate a cold shoulder toward you?

• What else occurs to you as you consider these questions?

• What insights do you have?

That Put My Back Up

According to one source, the derivation of the term "that put my back up" came into being in Britain in the 18th century and is derived from cats' habit of arching their backs when threatened or annoyed.[6] The expression continues to be used to describe the impact of being provoked by certain acts or deeds of another person. That is, not just cats, but some of us humans also demonstrate angry responses to perceived threats and things that annoy us, and so "put our backs up." As with the phrases "cold shoulder" and "chip on the shoulder," this one also reflects the fact that our bodies reveal our emotional reactions. It similarly conjures up a vivid image that provides different language to describe another somatic reaction to provocation.

Literally speaking, some of us react to something that challenges or provokes us by raising our shoulders, rounding or straightening our backs, and otherwise showing bodily reactions. There is usually no mistaking the posture, when observed, as anything but a defensive reaction. We may also use the expression "that put my back up" when we experience anger or other emotions internally in reaction to something another person says or does that offends us. So, we may not always show the impact outwardly at these times.

Though our backs may go up at any time in the conflict sequence, this reaction often appears early on when things begin to ignite. In any case, it is a good time to take the opportunity and examine what is happening. If this expression resonates for you—whether you are aware of your back going up when in conflict, or you have observed it in others—this series of questions will help to explore that experience.

QUESTIONS

- When your back goes up in conflict—literally or figuratively—what are you experiencing at these times?

- How would you describe how you appear at these times?

- How might a friend or family member who observes your back go up describe what they see?

- How do you think your reaction appears to the other person with whom there is discord that is different from your answers to the two previous questions? What may be the same?

- What sort of things put your back up? When answering this question, think of the last two or three times you could have used, or did use, this expression.

- When your back goes up, where does your heart go?

- When you have observed other people put their backs up when in conflict, how would you describe what you saw?

- What is the impact on you at these times (your answer to the above question)?

- How is putting your back up a useful conflict management technique? How is it not?

- If you want to stop putting your back up as a reaction to the other person or potential conflict situation, what might you do instead?

- What else occurs to you as you consider these questions?

- What insights do you have?

Making a Mountain Out of a Molehill

When we begin to experience irritation about something happening between another person and ourselves, our thoughts and feelings sometimes go to places that are not helpful for the situation and relationship. At these times, we are not always fully aware of what is happening, or the fact that our reactions may be escalating things. However, before we know it, our initial responses may take twists and turns that end up complicating matters. As they grow, our evolving perceptions may change from what they were in the beginning. And as things expand in our minds and hearts, we find ourselves more and more conflicted, confused, and upset.

Such a situation illustrates the essence of the expression "making a mountain out of a molehill." According to Wikipedia, the earliest recorded use of this phrase was in 1548, in a book by Nicholas Udall—thought to be one of the first people to use the expression. The historical meaning of this idiom had to do with "responding disproportionately to something—where a person exaggerates or makes too much of a minor issue."[7] This usage is generally consistent with the current meaning ascribed to this idiom.

Making a mountain out of a molehill is sometimes a reaction that we are aware of at some level of consciousness. Other times, we are not fully cognizant of how or why matters are growing bigger in our thoughts and feelings, and why we are becoming increasingly upset.

If you have a general tendency to exaggerate and imagine things being and becoming bigger than they are, you will find the questions on this topic especially pertinent. Even if you do not typically react this way, you may have done so in the past, and the topic arouses your curiosity. Or perhaps, this sort of reaction is happening at the current time, which is how the following questions are framed (though it is still helpful to consider past events to deconstruct this concept). In any case, it will help, when responding to these questions, to consider a specific situation about which something that started small is growing out of proportion.

QUESTIONS

- In the conflict you have in mind, what first provoked you (that is, what did the other person say or do, or not say or do, that led to an inner, negative reaction in you)?

- More specifically, what about that experience aroused your inner reaction?

- What is, or was, your inner reaction?

- Imagine that the initial provocation is an actual molehill. How would you describe what the molehill is, or was, made of? How else might you describe how it looks, or looked, when it began?

- What changed in your internal processing of things, or between you and the other person, that is resulting in the molehill's growth into a mountain?

- What is the mountain made of that the molehill wasn't?

- How are you experiencing the growth of the mountain that is different from your reaction to the molehill you described? In what ways is your reaction the same?

- Under what circumstances are you not as inclined to make a mountain out of a molehill? What relevance does your answer have to do with the particular situation you brought to mind?

- How might you stop the molehill from growing into a mountain? What conflict-masterful things could you do at this point if the mountain is appearing?

- How might you, in the future, stop yourself from making a mountain out of a molehill?

- What else occurs to you as you consider these questions?

- What insights do you have?

Jumping to Conclusions

The idiom "jumping to conclusions" essentially refers to a tendency to assume something as fact when there is not a clear reason to do so. Jumping to conclusions can easily exacerbate a conflict because we are operating on assumptions we do not know to be factual.

Conclusions may be about our perceptions of people's character, motives, attitude, and so on, based on their actions that irritate us. This sort of response—in which we attribute things to people without sure knowledge—may be due to factors such as our history with them or with similar situations or relationship dynamics. It may come from biases or stereotypes we have developed. It may be due to the habitual inclination to find fault or think the worst of people. We may tend to be negative and pessimistic in general, or be untrusting of others. Or, we may let our vulnerabilities, insecurities, and fears determine our interpretations.

Such variables as these and others tend to fuel the inclination to make meaning of something that is not necessarily applicable or possibly even relevant. Whatever the reasons, when we do not have facts to support the conclusions we reach, conflict often arises.

The following questions are designed to help bring to the surface whatever lies beneath your conclusions regarding another person in a specific situation. The questions will be especially useful if you are aware of a tendency to jump to conclusions, or if you are currently doing so about an interaction.

QUESTIONS

- In a situation in which you are jumping to a conclusion, what is your conclusion about the other person?

- What was the starting point before you reached that conclusion (your answer to the previous question)? What propelled the jump to the conclusion you reached?

- What makes your conclusion a realistic possibility? How may it not be absolutely realistic?

- If the conclusion you determined is correct, what does that mean for you? What does it mean for your relationship with the other person?

- If your conclusion is not correct, what does that mean for you? What does it mean for your relationship with the other person?

- What other possible conclusions might there be other than what you have considered so far?

- If this situation was told to you by someone else going through this experience, what thoughts, or what other conclusions, may occur to you to suggest that you have not contemplated as yet?

- What do you think occupies the space between your starting point and the conclusion you reached? How does what is in the space change your conclusion, if it does?

- What is your preferred conclusion? In what ways, if any, may that conclusion be possible despite the determination you initially made?

- What are some ways you can think of to refrain from jumping to conclusions in the future if you think there is benefit in doing so?

- What else occurs to you as you consider these questions?

- What insights do you have?

Making Assumptions

As with the tendency to jump to conclusions, figuring out from where and how our assumptions arise is not a straightforward exercise. Undoubtedly, our life experiences over time, our instincts, reasons why we say or do related things, explanations provided by family, friends, and colleagues, and other rationales have an impact on our interpretations.

Further, gossip we hear or participate in, the closeness of the particular relationship, the understanding and trust between us, how empathetic we are in general and specifically about the other person in this scenario, the degree to which we tend to judge others, how attuned we are to ourselves, and a wide range of other variables also influence our thinking and contribute to what we read into people's words, actions, behaviors, attitudes, and more.

Sometimes the meaning we give and what we assume about a statement or action by one person may differ from similar experiences with another person who says or does the same thing. That is, we may overlook, make excuses for, or smile at something done or said by a dear friend and not make negative assumptions about her or his motives, whereas we may read ill intent into the same statement or action by someone we don't know or like for some reason. Whatever the case, conflict easily arises from misinterpretations, and misinterpretations may even turn into accusations.

We know that unexplored attributions do not foster conflict intelligence and that this aspect of conflict, like others, has many layers to it. The next series of questions provide an opportunity to examine some of those attributions if you have a tendency to make assumptions or assign motives to others, or are doing so in a particular situation. (This topic has some similarities to **Jumping to Conclusions,** and the questions there may also help in your reflections here.)

QUESTIONS

- In a specific interaction in which you are interpreting someone's words or actions in negative ways, what did the person specifically say or do (or not say or do) that is having an adverse impact on you?

- For what reasons do you think she or he is saying or doing that?

- What is leading you to believe this is what she or he intended?

- What explanation might the other person provide about those actions or words that may not be consistent with the reasons you named (your answer to the second question, above)?

- If you have observed a friend saying or doing these same things or something similar, what other reason or reasons, if any, occur to you? If you have said or done the same sort of thing, what other reasons arise?

- What do you think would surprise the other person most about what you have assumed about her or his actions or words? What may surprise you about other possible explanations that she or he, or someone else, might suggest?

- If you think the person in this situation intended to cause a negative impact on you, why would that be the case?

- What do you suppose keeps you from checking out your assumptions with her or him? What is that hesitation about? What is likely to happen if you do not check out your assumptions?

- If you do check out your assumptions and find you accurately identified them, what impact will that have on you and your relationship with the other person? What may be the impact on you and the relationship if you are not accurate about your assumptions?

- What is your learning here about making assumptions that will help you in your efforts to strengthen your conflict intelligence?

- What else occurs to you as you consider these questions?

- What insights do you have?

More Explorations of Conflict Perceptions

Once we become irritated by another person, and especially if our feelings escalate with repeated interactions, it is challenging to drop the negative assumptions we conjure up about her or him and the motives we attribute. What also happens in many cases is that we get stuck in our positions and do not hear or clearly understand what is being said and why. Our assumptions grow as we become further entrenched and we lose perspective and a grasp on our feelings and thoughts—and what is going on for the other person. We do that and the other person does that, limiting the possibilities for clarifying, understanding, and possibly reconciling our differences.

As with making assumptions and jumping to conclusions, the quest for conflict mastery benefits from an exploration of any tendency to attribute negative interpretations of others and their words and deeds as soon as we are provoked. The objective of exploring this subject further here is to encourage consideration of other ways that help increase awareness about perceptions before acting on them—and to consider how you may be perceived too, to be able to unravel more effectively the ways in which perceptions impede the way forward.

For this set of questions, it is suggested that you examine a specific situation to which you are reacting and you are not sure whether your perceptions are 100 percent correct. Although there is no obligation to do so, if you select the scenario you explored for one or both of the previous topics (**Making Assumptions**, **Jumping to Conclusions**), this set of questions takes a slightly different approach and may further add to your exploration of conflict perceptions.

QUESTIONS

- What are your perceptions about the other person's contribution to the situation that has the potential for evolving between you?

- About what are you 100 percent certain regarding the other person's contribution? What part or parts of your perceptions about her or him may not be absolutely accurate?

- What negative motives may account for her or his actions or words? What positive ones may there be?

- What may the other person's perceptions be of you and your part in the conflict?

- What negative motives may she or he be attributing to you?

- With which part or parts of the other person's possible perceptions of you and your motives in the situation do you agree? With which part or parts of her or his possible perceptions of you and your motives do you disagree?

- What positive motives for your actions or words may she or he be unaware of or missing?

- If you were to start anew regarding the dynamic between you, what would you do differently? How would that change the other person's perceptions? What might she or he have done differently that would have changed your perceptions of her or him?

- What do you not know about the other person that, if you did know, might be helpful to better manage things between you? How might your answer(s) here be relevant to the assumptions you are making?

- What do you want to have happen in this situation that is not likely to happen because of your current perceptions of each other? How might you influence a more positive outcome?

- What else occurs to you as you consider these questions?

- What insights do you have?

Giving People the Benefit of the Doubt

One of the options we have about how to react to someone who provokes us is to give the person "the benefit of the doubt." This expression is reportedly derived from the legal phrase "reasonable doubt" first documented in 17th-century English law.[8] The phrase was said to refer to the degree of doubt required to acquit a criminal defendant, and was defined in terms of moral certainty. This expression continues to be commonly used when assessing criminal culpability. It is used in other contexts, too, such as when we are experiencing interpersonal conflict and attributing blame.

How does giving another person the benefit of the doubt apply in conflict situations? The expression may be relevant, for instance, when it comes to whether or not we blame the other person for something that offends us. If we give her or him the benefit of the doubt, we are being open to the possibility that maybe we are not absolutely correct in our fault-finding, and that there may be understandable and forgivable reasons for what is provoking us. Or, as discussed in **Jumping to Conclusions, Making Assumptions**, and **More Explorations of Conflict Perceptions**, it may be we attribute negative interpretations, make assumptions, or jump to conclusions based on our perceptions of others' actions, words, and motives, although we do not know for sure that they apply.

If we give the benefit of the doubt, we are able to reframe what we are attributing or, at least, to drop our attachment to our initial assumptions. In essence, we can consider other possible reasons for people's conduct.

The following questions will help to flush out a tendency to blame where there is a lack of absolute certainty about the reasons for the other person's actions or words. These questions will also help to generate thinking about alternative rationales that may be feasible—giving the other person the benefit of the doubt. Doing so may ultimately prevent escalation of unnecessary conflict. **Understanding Why We Blame** in Chapter 4 also explores aspects of fault-finding that are relevant here.

QUESTIONS

- When you consider a situation in which you are blaming another person for something, with what specifically are you finding fault?

- Why do you suppose she or he is doing or saying that?

- If the other person overheard your response, with what do you know for sure she or he would disagree? With what are you certain she or he would agree?

- What alternative or additional reasons might the other person give you for saying or doing what was said or done?

- What sounds reasonable about the other person's possible answer(s) to the previous question? What does not resonate?

- What other plausible reasons might you suggest to someone else in this situation?

- If you were to give the other person the benefit of the doubt for anything, what might that be?

- Why that or those things?

- What positive feelings do you experience, if any, when you consider giving her or him the benefit of the doubt? What about giving the benefit of the doubt does not work for you? Why is that so?

- Under what circumstances do you usually give people the benefit of the doubt? What difference does it make whether or not you give the other person the benefit of the doubt?

- What else occurs to you as you consider these questions?

- What insights do you have?

Speaking Up

One of the things that complicates conflict and leads to bad experiences is the inability to speak up, voice our needs, stand up for ourselves, express our feelings, and explain or defend our perspective. Even if we usually have the ability to do any of these things, the nature of some conflicts, and the dynamics between certain people and ourselves, may impede our confidence and courage at times.

Though a fear of conflict, possible repercussions, and other reasons get in the way of effectively initiating and engaging in potentially difficult discussions, not speaking up can lead to discord. At the very least, when we do not speak up we experience internal dissension, and that has a negative impact on us and our relationship with the other person. And these sorts of feelings tend to build up over time.

In reality, certain situations and dynamics between us and others are more challenging to manage. For some of us, speaking up does not come easily under most circumstances, much less a potentially fractious interaction. Our emotions, individual conflict styles and experiences, and self-limiting beliefs and behaviors all add other layers of complexity. Composure and confidence typically plummet at these times along with self-esteem, such that speaking up becomes even less likely.

If you have challenges finding and keeping your voice when in conflict, these questions will help you explore these and other possible ways to overcome them. Being able to speak up is undoubtedly to our benefit if we use the pertinent skills before conflict emerges. However, honing proficiencies for effectively expressing ourselves is a good plan for use anywhere along the conflict trajectory.

QUESTIONS

- What does the expression "speaking up" mean to you? In your view, what three words best describe what you experience when you do not speak up when there is growing discord between you and another person? What sorts of things go through your head at these times?

- When you consider a particular situation in which you are not speaking up, what specifically is keeping you from doing so? Why is that so?

- What is not speaking up costing you?

- What is the worst thing you can imagine happening if you do speak up?

- On a scale of 1 to 5, 5 being "absolutely" and 1 being "absolutely not," how realistic is the possibility that the worst thing you just described could happen if you speak up? If your answer is 5, what makes it so? If your answer is 4 or less, what does the rating mean?

- In the particular situation you are considering here, what three words describe how you will feel if you express what you want to say and your messages get across? What do you envision as the best-case scenario if you speak up?

- What are the main messages you would express if you did speak up in that situation? How might you begin a dialogue, if you gain more skills and confidence to speak up, that is most likely to lead toward the feelings and best-case scenario you just described (your answers to the previous question)?

- What skills and abilities do you want to work on to help carry through this conversation? What else do you think would help you find your voice?

- What do you want to learn about yourself to facilitate your proficiency in this area in future conflicts?

- What inner resources do you know you already have to be able to express yourself in this and future conflicts, based on previous experiences when you have been able to speak up?

- What else occurs to you as you consider these questions?

- What insights do you have?

You Make Me So Angry

For a number of reasons, the expression, "You make me so angry" (or sad, disappointed, depressed, and so on) does not quite work. Sentences that begin this way indicate that the speaker believes the other person has the power and ability to cause the emotions the speaker feels. Such statements essentially blame someone else for something only we have the power and ability to control and regulate. This topic explores our own power when it comes to emotions we experience in conflict.

This by no means suggests that it is not necessary to explore the feelings we experience in response to another person's actions or words. Our negative reactions to what someone does or says usually reflect that we perceive something meaningful to us is being challenged. By examining these reactions, we are better able to identify and understand what needs, values, and beliefs are of such major importance that they motivate strong emotions in us when we sense another person challenges or threatens them. Further, thinking out what drives our emotions, in each of our conflicts, strengthens our ability to regulate them through increased awareness about what we are experiencing and why.

The level of consciousness that arises from exploring what lies beneath our emotional reactions also helps to preempt forays into unnecessary conflict and interactions that may be managed more effectively. We may accomplish this, for instance, not only by gaining more clarity about what incites our reactions, but also by considering what is driving the other person's reactions. Insights such as these—about why certain actions compel strong feelings in us and the other person—facilitate the route to conflict mastery.

Here are some questions that help such an exploration by focusing on a specific emotion you are experiencing, or have experienced, in a conflict. (This aspect is further explored in Chapter 3 under the topic **Understanding Heightened Emotions When in Conflict**.)

QUESTIONS

- If you are making a statement that begins with, "She or he makes me so _____ (angry, upset, sad…)" about a person's words, actions, and so on in a specific conflict, what is one emotion you might use to fill in this blank?

- What happened, or is happening, that resulted in that emotion?

- In what way(s) does the other person cause _____ (whatever emotion you answered in the first question)?

- What part or parts of your previous answer describes your perception of the other person's intention(s)? Or, if your perception about the other person's intention(s) is not included in your answer to the previous question, what do you think it is (or they are)?

- If you do not think the other person intended to cause the emotions you referred to (in the first question in this series), what reasons might there be for her or his actions or words?

- What emotion, if any, comes up for you when you consider those possible reasons (your answer to the previous question)?

- If you believe the other person has the ability and power to "make" you feel what you did, what sorts of things foster this belief?

- If you believe the other person did not actually *make* you feel what you experienced, how does that belief change things, if at all?

- What ability and power do you believe you have regarding your reactions to the other person in this scenario? What other strengths do you already have to be able to respond in conflict-masterful ways?

- Generally speaking, what sorts of abilities and power do you have and intend to use going forward when other people's actions and words negatively affect you?

- What else occurs to you as you consider these questions?

- What insights do you have?

Preparing to Initiate a Conflict Conversation

Being involved in conflict-related conversations is a common happenstance. Whether we initiate them or others do, many of us experience some degree of angst in anticipation of communications perceived to be potentially contentious. Fears often surface, as does a range of other unsettling reactions that relate to our insecurities and vulnerabilities. Whatever we dread about such conversations has the potential for reducing our confidence and ability to communicate.

One of the other consequences of being apprehensive about raising conflictual matters (even ones that may only possibly be so) is that we tend to put them off. Or, we blurt out something hurtful, in awkward ways, or at inappropriate times, or when the other person is not ready and open to listen. Because one or more of these approaches may result in counterproductive communications and unnecessary conflict, it helps to give careful consideration about how best to proceed.

Preparation is key. That is, becoming masterful at initiating (or responding to) communications when we begin to notice dissension requires stepping back early on and engaging in thoughtful preparation. It means being purposeful about what we are hoping to achieve and what it takes to do so. It means thinking out what we want to be most prepared for. It means facing our fears about the situation, including our worries about how the other person may react and how we will manage such reactions if our concerns become reality. It means considering what other variables need to be contemplated to be able to plan the optimal interaction, as much as possible.

Taking a methodical and reflective approach before entering into conversations that may become problematic, then, helps in many ways. For instance, by doing so we gain distance from the situation and the emotions that drive us to react. We take time to consider different perspectives, and get clearer on our perceptions and assumptions including those we need to check out. We envision and practice optional responses in the event we are challenged. We consider possible solutions to the issues in dispute. And with all this focused preparation, we build conflict intelligence and mastery.

The following questions are designed to help you prepare for a potentially challenging conversation that you aim to initiate and engage in with conflict mastery.

QUESTIONS

- What is the outcome you want to achieve in this conversation? What are the key messages you want to convey to be able to achieve that outcome? What else do you intend to say or do to help facilitate reaching the result you want?

- What outcome may the other person want?

- What of the other person's messages do you want to be most prepared for? How do you want to respond to those messages in a way that reflects conflict mastery?

- To what extent do you want to strive for a result that is mutually acceptable? What result might that be?

- If you want things to resolve in a mutually satisfactory way, what will a collaborative approach sound like?

- How do you want to be, and be perceived, during this conversation? What tone, manner, or body language do you intend to have in order to come across the way you want? What will you *not* say or do in this conversation because it is not aligned with your intentions?

- What is your biggest fear about initiating this conversation? What is likely *not* realistic about that happening? What is likely realistic about that fear? What is the optimal way to prepare for that possibility?

- How do you want to be in relation to the other person when this conversation is over? How do you want to feel about yourself?

- What do you know from observing others and your own positive experiences with other interpersonal conflicts that will help you interact the way you want to in this conversation?

- What other conflict-masterful ways of being will guide you to interact in this conversation the way you want?

- What else occurs to you as you consider these questions?

- What insights do you have?

Boundary Considerations in a Conflict Conversation

This topic is linked to the previous one—the intention-setting nature of planning a conflict-related conversation. Boundary considerations require giving even more thought to the approaches that will help achieve your desired outcome, and more particularly, what you plan to stay away from saying or doing. That is, as discussed in Chapter 1 and in the topic **The Platinum Moment of Choice in Conflict** in this chapter, our reactions, attitudes, and manner are all choices we have. Considering what not do or say—because it could cross a line for the other person and derail the dialogue altogether—is therefore crucial.

We all have limits of tolerance—referred to here as "boundaries"—regarding what constitutes acceptable ways of interacting. Sometimes when others cross our boundaries, or we cross theirs, the result is a breakdown of communications, negatively affecting the discussion, including how to reconcile matters, if that is the objective (or part) of the conversation. Even when we know there is a risk of crossing a line, being well prepared to deliver difficult messages and effectively receive and respond to the other person's reaction remains a conflict-mastery objective. Much of the time, we are not aware of what may push things too far, and this means striving as best we can to anticipate and prepare for a range of possibilities.

The following questions invite you to consider the other person's possible limits of tolerance to be able to keep a pending conversation on track, even if crossing a line is inevitable and necessary. (Reconsidering the questions in **Preparing to Initiate a Conflict Conversation** may help as you further explore the elements of effective conflict conversations here.)

QUESTIONS

- When you consider the communication you are planning, what might you say or do, based on your knowledge of the other person, that may push her or him too far? If you do not know (or cannot speculate possible answers), what sorts of things might cross a boundary if you imagine yourself as the other person in the conversation?

- What may that thing (or those things) say about what is important to the other person that you want to consider in the dialogue?

- What concerns do you have about what may happen if you cross the other person's boundary?

- What do you want to get out in the open that has some boundary risks? How may you best present that (or those)?

- If the other person's boundary is crossed, in what ways might that help things? How might it hurt things?

- What will you do to handle matters—in conflict-masterful ways—if the other person reacts strongly after experiencing that you crossed her or his boundary?

- Regarding the conflict between you, what do you think the other person might say or do in the conversation that would cross your boundary or boundaries?

- How might you describe your boundary or boundaries (from the previous question) in more detail? What does this say about what is important to you?

- How might having your boundary crossed help things? How might it hurt things?

- In what conflict-masterful ways might you respond if the other person's messages or ways of delivering them cross your boundaries?

- What else occurs to you as you consider these questions?

- What insights do you have?

Preparing to Respond in a Conflict Conversation

Because some of us are regularly involved in communications that have the potential for becoming combative, emotional, inflammatory, argumentative, and so on, we know that some responses work better than others. When someone initiates a conversation of this nature, it can catch us off guard to the extent that we do not respond in ways that work well for engaging in a constructive dialogue. Being able to participate effectively in discussions that may become divisive when someone else initiates them is an indicator of conflict mastery, just as it is when we are the initiator. Similarly, postponing the interaction until we are ready, while at the same time not being perceived as ignoring the other person's initiative, is another sign.

Determining the optimal time to engage in communications that someone else initiates can be challenging, and timing is not a choice that we usually think we have. Nevertheless, preparing to respond in a respectful and thoughtful way requires, among other things, being purposeful and careful about when to do so, not only how.

Suggesting alternative timing when not ready, for instance, may sound like, "Thank you for approaching me on this. Let's get a time that works for both of us to do so." Or, "I hear how important this is and I want to talk about it, too. I just need to think things through first. When else are you available?" Statements of this nature—using your words and manner of speaking, of course—often help deflect negative energy and the urgency being experienced if feeling pressed by the other person. This is especially so if her or his approach triggers a negative reaction.

The following questions will help you focus and prepare for the occasions when another person initiates a potentially contentious and challenging conversation. These questions (along with those in **Preparing to Initiate a Conflict Conversation** and **Boundary Considerations in a Conflict Conversation**) will increase awareness about how to facilitate and participate in a constructive dialogue with the objective of preempting unnecessary conflict.

QUESTIONS

- When you are the initiator of a conversation aiming to prevent unnecessary conflict, what is it like for you? In what similar ways do you suppose the other person who is inviting a dialogue with you may be experiencing the role of initiator? What do you imagine may be different for her or him?

- What is a conflict-masterful way for you to respond when someone else initiates a conversation, if you are not ready at the time you are approached?

- If you think about a specific situation where discord is present and the other person wants to discuss it, what are the possible opportunities for you in having this conversation? What opportunities may there be for her or him?

- What risks are possible for you? What risks may there be for the other person?

- Related to this specific situation, what would you want to clarify? What clarification might the other person want?

- What do you want to be most careful about in your response—for instance, approaches that have not worked before for you, or for others you have observed, that you do not want to repeat? What has worked well for you, or for others you have observed, that you want to repeat?

- For this situation, what are the skills you want to hone to be able to respond effectively? What else is important that you want or need to be most prepared for in this particular conversation?

- How will you know when you are ready to engage in this conversation?

- Going forward, what do you consider will be the main challenges for you when someone else initiates a conflict-related conversation? How else may you best prepare for these challenges that you have not yet considered here?

- Based on your reflections and answers here, what are some other best practices you plan to use when responding to someone else who initiates a potentially difficult conversation?

- What else occurs to you as you consider these questions?

- What insights do you have?

CHAPTER THREE

During Conflict

During Conflict—Some Preliminary Thoughts to Consider

When we are in the midst of conflict, different parts of our being and ways of coping commonly emerge. Reacting in such moments frequently brings out behaviors about which we later agonize. Some are familiar to us, and some are so uncharacteristic that we hardly recognize them. Some reflect what we think is appropriate for the situation based on our history and other influences. Some are guided by our inner voices stumbling over words, or soothing us to calm down, or telling us what to say or do. Some show the dark emotions we try to suppress but which may seep out anyway, sometimes in large waves.

Other reactions emerge, too. We may yell and curse. Or, we may shut down and be unresponsive. We may yield to the other person or fight back. We slide down the slippery slope of the three Ds—**D**emonizing, **D**ehumanizing, and **D**egrading. We say things we cannot take back and later regret. We may experience a range of somatic reactions, too. Our heart may pound harder, our face redden, our jaw and hands clench, our fingers fidget, and so on.

Chapter 1 talked about how, in the heat of interpersonal conflict, it is often difficult to think clearly, and our creative and problem-solving skills may be compromised. Though we may make our best efforts to cooperate and collaborate, once we become embroiled in an interaction many of us lose ourselves within it. That is, we seem to lose our perspective, and get caught up in our emotions and those of the other person. We lose our empathy and our connection with the other person and ourselves.

Ideally, in the middle of conflict we gather the wherewithal to take deep breaths and not react. We request time and space to calm ourselves and think things out. We consider what is upsetting us and where the other person is coming from. We reflect on how to make our communications more constructive. We manage ourselves in ways that align with our values and how we prefer to interact at these times.

Until we become conflict masterful, it is difficult to imagine applying these skills mid-conflict. It is also difficult to recognize that we have an opportunity at these times to better understand the other person and ourselves and what is important to both of us. That is, while conflict is in progress, such opportunities reveal themselves when we lower our defenses and listen with intention. It is in these moments that we have the chance to learn what we may do and say to prevent our disputes from escalating unnecessarily, resulting in regrets that weigh us down after our conflicts are over. What is more, *during* conflict we have an opportunity to make conscious choices about how we want to be and be perceived. The reality is, there we do not demonstrate these and other proficiencies that we will be able to enact once we strengthen our knowledge, skills, and abilities to engage more effectively in conflict.

Post-conflict topics are discussed in detail in Chapter 4. However, it is important to emphasize here that the root of lingering vestiges of our interactions often plant themselves *during* our disputes. That is, after our conflicts are ostensibly over, we may look back with guilt and remorse—wishing we had said or done something differently. We may continually blame the other person for words or actions that hurt us. We feel shame and mourn lost opportunities. Our "shoulds" emerge too, and may sound like this: "Maybe I should have kept my mouth shut"; "Maybe I should have told him about other things he does that irritate me"; "I should have just told her the truth"; and so on.

These sorts of repercussions and others—after the fact—remind us of our vulnerabilities when we are ill prepared to face the various challenges and uncertainties that emerge while our interpersonal conflicts are in progress. It helps at these times to remind ourselves that we are reacting because something is important to us, and also that we are doing our best to meet our needs and defend what is meaningful to us—as is the other person. Indeed, our "best," and theirs, may at times come out sloppy, ill-conceived, loud, obnoxious, hurtful, and unproductive. That is why many of us try to improve our ways of engaging in conflict. While it takes two to sustain a conflict, it takes only one to change the paradigm.

Because continuous opportunities for learning present themselves in the heat of the moment, this chapter is devoted to the quest for conflict intelligence and mastery during situations in which we become embroiled. These may occur spontaneously, when we least expect them. The topics, which reflect many common scenarios that occur during conflict, essentially invite you to identify ways to step back—literally and figuratively—and reflect before responding. You will also be asked to contemplate different ways of being in, and approaching, conflict to make it a more positive experience.

The Conflict Iceberg

The image of an iceberg has been used as a metaphor for conflict,[1] and it makes an interesting visual when we consider the various elements of our disputes. The image is based on the premise that part of what is happening during a conflict is above the surface and another part is below the "water line."

The tip of the iceberg—obvious to the other person, us, and others—represents the discord. This is essentially what the issue seems to be about, the positions we are taking, and the apparent impact of the conflict on us. Then, there is the mass of ice that is underneath the water line. In the conflict analogy, this part contains such elements as our hopes, expectations, needs, values, beliefs, interests, and emotions. They—along with our individual and collective histories, which we also bring to our disputes—lie hidden beneath the surface.

While for all intents and purposes, the underlying portion of our conflicts appears to be unnoticed, its components have an enormous impact on us and our interactions with others. Indeed, they are an integral part of the conflict and who we are within it, within ourselves, and within the relationship. (Aspects of the conflict iceberg referred to here are also considered in this chapter under the topic **Positions and Interests**.)

In some conflict circumstances, it may seem best to leave underlying aspects unexplored. However, we are likely to miss opportunities that might benefit us, our relationship, and the course of the conflict, if we do not bring to the surface much of what lies below the idiomatic water line. For instance, without such an examination, we miss gaining an understanding of the dynamics that are contributing to the conflict. We miss obtaining a fuller perspective on what is meaningful to us and to the other person, and why. We miss discovering whether there is common ground and a way to reconcile our differences and the issues in dispute.

The following questions aim to increase your understanding of the dynamics and their impact through considering a conflict in which you see only the tip of the iceberg. The questions may also "defrost" some other significant aspects that will reveal ideas about what might be done to resolve matters and reconcile the relationship, if that is what you want.

QUESTIONS

- What is above the surface and fully evident to you in the conflict you have in mind? What do you think is evident to the other person? What might bystanders see or hear that is not included in your answers so far?

- What lies beneath the iceberg that is evident to you, but is not likely evident to the other person, such as your hopes, needs, and expectations? Describing the specifics of these elements is important here.

- What have you shared with the other person so far regarding the impact of the conflict on you? What do you *not* want to express about the impact of the conflict on you that lies below the surface, if that is the case? Why are you keeping it there? How might expressing the impact be helpful?

- What else are you keeping below the surface? Why is that so? In what ways might it (or those things) be important to how the conflict unfolds? What might the other person miss by not knowing what you are keeping below the surface?

- What might be going on for the other person that is not evident to you, such as her or his hopes, needs, and expectations? Try to be specific about what you think they are.

- For what reasons might the other person want to leave the things you named—in response to the previous question—below the surface? What else do you think she or he may be keeping there?

- From what you are able to observe and glean, what impact is the conflict having on the other person? What might she or he be experiencing but keeping below the surface? If that is the case, why do you think this is so? In what ways might the answers here, and to the preceding questions about the other person—if they are shared with you—affect how the conflict unfolds?

- What do you imagine the best possible outcome of this conflict might be for you? What makes that outcome the best? What best possible outcome might the other person want? Why may that be important to her or him?

- What do you think needs to "defrost" and come to the surface for you and the other person to be able to reach a mutually acceptable outcome—if that is what you want?

- Whether or not you are aiming for a mutually agreeable outcome, what about the iceberg concept is helpful in analyzing this conflict? What, from this series of questions, stands out as helpful pieces of learning for future conflicts?

- What else occurs to you as you consider these questions?

- What insights do you have?

Making Others Wrong

One of the things that often happens when we are in the middle of an interpersonal conflict is that we perceive the difference between the other person's perspective and ours is a matter of right and wrong. That is, we are right and the other person is wrong! Of course, that might well be the other person's perspective, too.

This topic does not address right and wrong from a moral or ethical point of view. Rather, it explores how people engaged in relational conflicts perceive each other's disparate views. Those and a variety of other incompatibilities—including how we are communicating—can cause us to make "rightness" and "wrongness" judgments about each other. Such polarities can fuel our emotions and pull us apart.

When dynamics of this nature occur, our interactions commonly deteriorate into positional and personal disagreements in which we make the other person wrong by defending our viewpoint as though there were no room for alternative perspectives. As things become more inflamed, we tend to express ourselves and our opinions with heightened passion. Sometimes our arguments and the reasons for them are not even comprehensible, and all that resounds are "right and wrong" sentiments. (The topic **Positions and Interests** later in this chapter also discusses opposing perspectives, in a different way.)

When both of us are entrenched in our own beliefs of what is right and wrong, it is a good time to call a few points to mind. To begin with, declaring ourselves right and the other person wrong does not advance resolution, reconcile the relationship, clear the air, or achieve other positive outcomes. Also, acknowledging the other person's views of what constitutes right and wrong does not mean we have to give up our beliefs about what constitutes right or wrong for us. Further, we are under no obligation to agree with the other person's viewpoint. However, it is important to recognize that we both hold perspectives that are personally meaningful to us, though they are different—perhaps very different—from each other's.

In the quest for conflict mastery, it helps to ask ourselves this question: Does our view of rightness have to preclude the other person's view of what rightness is for herself or himself? There are conflict-masterful ways to approach our differences—if our goal is to accomplish mutually acceptable results—and this topic explores what those methods might be. As Jalāl ad-Dīn Rumi wrote: "Out beyond ideas of wrongdoing and rightdoing, there is a field. I'll meet you there."[2]

The following self-reflective questions will be of particular interest if you are experiencing "right and wrong" assertions in a conflict with another person that are proving to be counterproductive. These questions invite you to ponder the open space that lies somewhere between your two viewpoints in order to consider whether there may be a meeting place. (A related topic, discussed later in this chapter, is **Agreeing to Disagree**.)

QUESTIONS

- When you consider the disagreement between yourself and the other person, what do you believe the conflict is about? What makes your view "right"? What makes your viewpoint "wrong" according to the other person?

- What is the other person's perspective of what the conflict is about? What makes her or his viewpoint "wrong" to you?

- What is "right" about the other person's view as far as she or he is concerned that you do not agree with? What, if anything, might you acknowledge as having some rightness to her or his point of view?

- What seems to be getting in the way of the other person's acknowledging or understanding your perspective, if that is the case, even if she or he does not agree with it? What might be getting in the way of your acknowledging her or his perspective, if that is the case, even if you do not agree with it? What else may be going on within the conflict dynamic that might account for your respective challenges in acknowledging or understanding each other's perspective?

- What have you not shared with the other person that might be relevant to the conflict and important for her or him to know? What do you want to know that the other person has not shared—that you consider relevant and important?

- What difference does it make whether or not you attach the words "right" and "wrong" to your disparate views?

- If you are able to imagine the two of you acknowledging what is most important to each other about your differences, what would you want the other person to acknowledge? What do you think she or he would want you to acknowledge?

- Now that you have considered your answers about this matter, what, if anything, might be more acceptable about the other person's viewpoint than you initially thought?

- What might remain to be discovered in the area between the "right" and "wrong" positions you and the other person are taking on your different viewpoints that you have not considered yet? Where, if anyplace, might you ultimately meet in the field beyond your "ideas of wrongdoing and rightdoing"?

- If you were to identify something that might help to begin to reconcile your differences, if that is what you want, what would that be?

- What else occurs to you as you consider these questions?

- What insights do you have?

Name-Calling

Even though we know that name-calling is an infantile reaction to feeling offended or a way of offending another person, there are times in the heat of anger that we realize we have resorted to this form of blaming. Or, the other person has done so and we hear her or him verbally attacking us with derogatory names. Names called under such circumstances are typically insulting, mean, belittling, demeaning, and sometimes even discriminatory.

You may remember the expression "sticks and stones may break my bones, but names will never hurt me," formerly (and perhaps still) said in response to verbal bullying in grade school playgrounds. The meaning is evident and is described by one resource as a "response to an insult, implying that 'You might be able to hurt me by physical force but not by insults.'"[3]

Though this childhood phrase suggests otherwise, names that are expressed in anger do hurt, often deeply. Name-calling is full of negative attributions that serve to polarize and even create a power imbalance that precludes effective conflict engagement and communications. Frequently, name-calling leaves indelible marks by echoing indefinitely in the ears of those on the receiving end long after the disagreement is over.

For some of us, calling people names has become a habit when we are in conflict. It may occur when our level of frustration grows or when we lose our words and ability to express ourselves. For some, it is a purposeful put-down—intended to hurt. For others, it is an attempt to "win" a fight, or it may be used as a way to shut down the interaction. **When You Throw Dirt, You Lose Ground** and **Criticizing**—the next two topics in this chapter—also relate to this manner of coping with conflict.

From the point of view of developing conflict intelligence, it is worth exploring the feeling and words behind name-calling and the moments that incite its use. The following questions help to examine this way of reacting during conflict—whether it is impulsive, or a tendency, or an occasional way of managing a difficult situation when all else fails.

QUESTIONS

- If you name-call at times, what name(s) did you use in the last conflict when you did so?

- Why did you choose that name or those particular names?

- What motivated you to name-call—that is, to what specifically were you reacting?

- What emotions were you experiencing about the other person when you called her or him that name (names)? What were you feeling about the conflict between you? What were you feeling about yourself?

- What was the observable impact on the other person when you called her or him the name(s) you referred to in the first question?

- What was the message or messages you wanted to convey by using that name or those names?

- What message(s) got across, from what you can tell? If someone else heard the name or names you called, what messages might they have heard or inferred that you were conveying?

- What did you achieve by name-calling? What were you hoping might happen by name-calling that did not happen?

- What did you need or expect from the other person that she or he was not delivering at the time you name-called? What stopped you from expressing that need or expectation instead? If you were to frame what you needed or expected as a request, what would that sound like?

- In the future, if you find yourself beginning to name-call, what conflict-masterful approaches might you take instead?

- What else occurs to you as you consider these questions?

- What insights do you have?

When You Throw Dirt, You Lose Ground

Some of us turn our negative energy inward when we find ourselves becoming reactive during conflict. Some of us turn it outward—on the other person. Some of us do both. Examples of turning our energy outward may be by "throwing dirt" in the form of **Name-Calling** (just discussed) or **Criticizing** (discussed next), gossiping about the other person, and saying mean-spirited things to and about her or him. The phrase "When you throw dirt, you lose ground,"[4] also called "mud-slinging," is a figurative way to describe what happens when we do these things. That is, when we criticize, gossip, name-call, and so on, we succeed only in "losing ground," which is a military idiom meaning to lose your advantage.[5]

Throwing dirt, in whatever guise it takes, usually backfires in a number of ways. Examples include the other person's refusing to engage with us at all. Or, she or he reacts with equally unproductive actions and words, perpetuating even more discord and unnecessary conflict. Matters do not get resolved. We become depleted. We feel ashamed about our way of coping and ruminate at length. We realize the uselessness of this approach—with no recourse, having offended and alienated the other person. We lose self-respect, along with ground we hoped to gain in the conflict, and we find ourselves in a deep hole we dug by "throwing dirt."

Some other examples of how throwing dirt backfires: People to whom we complain about the other person do not provide support. Some may find our own actions in the dispute, as we convey them, to be petty and mean. As a result, they might defend the other person, or react in other ways that even lead to conflict with us, too. As with the other possible consequences, when these sorts of things happen, ground is lost not only with the other person. We may lose ground within ourselves, too, in the form of diminished confidence and self-esteem.

If you have found yourself throwing dirt in a current conflict, have done so in the past, or if someone is throwing or has thrown dirt at you, this set of questions will be especially relevant. (You may even find some of the questions pertinent to the dirt you throw in your *thoughts* about another person, whether or not conflict has evolved. Even just thinking negative thoughts about others contributes adversely to the interrelational dynamic between you.) The topic **Understanding Why We Blame**, in Chapter 4, is also relevant to this situation.

QUESTIONS

- When you consider a specific conflict incident, what did you say or do (or think) that constitutes "throwing dirt"?

- What motivated you to throw dirt in the way you just described?

- What ground did you lose in the conflict by throwing dirt? What ground did you lose with the other person? In what ways did you gain ground with the conflict? With the other person?

- What was the preferred outcome you were hoping for in this conflict? What happened that was consistent with your hopes? What was contrary to what you had hoped?

- Instead of throwing dirt, what could you have done or said differently that might have resulted in your preferred outcome?

- In your answer to the previous question, what specifically would have taken the place of dirt?

- When you consider a situation in which someone threw or is throwing dirt at you, what did she or he specifically say or do? How did this dirt-throwing affect you?

- What ground did the other person lose regarding any issues in dispute? What was lost in your relationship? What other ground did the other person lose by throwing dirt at you? What did she or he gain?

- How might you describe the ground you prefer to stand on when you are in a conflict?

- What would it take for you to make the ground feel as you would prefer (your answer to the previous question) when you are in conflict? How might you make, or could you have made, that happen in conflict-masterful ways in the situation you described here where you are or were throwing dirt? In what conflict-masterful ways might you respond, or might you have responded, in the other scenario where you are or were on the receiving end of the other person's dirt-throwing?

- What else occurs to you as you consider these questions?

- What insights do you have?

Criticizing

Criticism takes different forms and tends to exacerbate conflict and derail conversations, preventing them from evolving in a productive manner. Examples may be finding fault when others' viewpoints do not suit us or our opinions. **Name-Calling**, put-downs, "dirt-throwing," and otherwise blaming people for their ideas, actions, personality, and so on, are also forms of criticism. Similarly, criticizing may be demonstrated by micromanaging, and by continually correcting things others say or do. Having a dismissive attitude, and being sarcastic, belittling, controlling, patronizing, and condescending, may all be experienced as criticism, too. Sometimes we do not criticize verbally, but our facial and body language speak for us.

For some of us, criticizing is a strategy for maintaining control or managing hurt, anger, and other emotions. We may criticize when we experience push-back of our perspectives. We may choose criticism to be in control, to make our point, to "win" a disagreement, or to undermine the other person and her or his opinions, needs, beliefs, and interests. Criticizers themselves may lack self-esteem and be self-critical, and criticizing others makes them feel more powerful. Or, we may genuinely dispute another person's perspective, or how she or he is acting, and choose criticism instead of more conflict-masterful approaches.

By criticizing—however we do it—we may be seen as demonstrating intolerance, judgmentalism, lack of flexibility, and a need to be right (see **Making Others Wrong**, earlier in this chapter). Criticizers also seem to have trouble separating the person from the real crux of the situation, adding to the negative dynamic. This means our differences become increasingly personal. It often seems, when this happens, that criticism breeds criticism. That is, once one of us commits one or more of the three Ds—**D**emonizing, **D**ehumanizing, and **D**egrading—discussed in the preliminary thoughts at the beginning of this chapter—it serves to incite the other person, who reacts with criticism back. Inevitably, we then both spiral downward in our interaction.

If you tend to criticize during a conflict or have done so in a specific situation, this is an opportunity to explore your reaction further. If someone has criticized you in a conflict, there are also some questions that provide a different way of looking at that situation.

QUESTIONS

- When you consider the last time you criticized someone during a conflict, what was the conflict? About what, specifically, were you being critical?

- What bothered you most about the other person's actions, words, and so on that resulted in your criticism? What were you experiencing at the time (feeling, thinking) about the other person?

- What, specifically, did you say by way of criticizing? How did the other person respond?

- If the other person became defensive in response to your criticism, what did you hear her or him defend?

- What were you aiming to accomplish with your criticism? How did you succeed in doing so? What did you *not* achieve that you had hoped to?

- What did you need or want the other person to say or do in that situation instead that you would *not* have criticized? How would you have interacted differently with her or him in that case?

- If you were to frame your criticism as a request, how would that sound?

- When you consider a situation in which someone criticized you during a conflict, what was that like for you? (If this happened in the same situation just discussed, it may be helpful to use that example here.) What do you suppose the other person needed or wanted from you at the time that you were not delivering?

- What request might the other person have made of you pertaining to the substance of the criticism that you would have been less likely to react negatively to? How might you have responded differently in this case?

- Looking back now on your answers to the above questions, what two new things have you learned, or been reminded of, about the use of criticism?

- What else occurs to you as you consider these questions?

- What insights do you have?

Understanding Heightened Emotions When in Conflict

Experiencing emotions is a natural part of being in conflict. Among other things, emotions reflect how important certain matters are to us and to each other, and the impact on us when we perceive a challenge or threat to them. Understanding the circumstances that lead to our heightened emotions in the midst of a conflict, and considering how best to express our feelings, are not always easy to do. Conflict mastery is, in part, about regulating our emotions at these times, and finding ways to share the impact without derailing the conversation.

When we find ourselves reacting in a conflict situation, it is an opportune time to listen with care and compassion to ourselves, to hear what is going on for us. It is especially helpful to name the specific words that describe what we are experiencing. Doing so helps us distance ourselves from the emotional part of the conflict dynamic. We are then better able to identify what activated our heightened emotions, and as a consequence, we are likely better able to regulate them.

Once our emotions are less active, the ability to reflect on the conflict dynamic increases. With growing awareness, we gain more trust in our instincts. We are more open to considering different perspectives, and our negative energy wanes all the more. Initial reactions turn into more reflective responses, including a clearer focus on resolving, or at least discussing, what is going on between us.

The questions on this topic are essentially designed to help you gain more clarity regarding your emotions during conflict, and to consider what it takes to regulate them. Several topics in Chapter 2—**Bottling Things Up, Conflict Jitters,** and **You Make Me So Angry**—discuss emotions that become aroused *before* conflict. In this chapter, **Getting Revved Up, Fears About Tears, Fears About Being in Conflict, Yelling When in Conflict,** and **The Conflict Groan** discuss emotions *during* conflict.

QUESTIONS

- When you consider a current dispute or the last time you were in one, what specifically did the other person say or do (or not say or do) that heightened negative emotions in you?

- What three words most accurately describe the emotions you are, or were, experiencing during the interaction?

- How does, or did, having those emotions otherwise affect you? How did you manifest those emotions in that dispute? If there are, or were, emotions you were not expressing outwardly, what were they? For what reasons are or were you keeping them inside?

- Which of your emotions are you sure the other person is aware of? How did they affect her or him, from what you could tell or observe? What other important emotions that you are experiencing do you want her or him to recognize?

- What do you understand about the reasons for your heightened emotions in this dispute? What do you *not* understand about the emotions you are, or were, experiencing? What do your instincts tell you about why your emotions heightened, if you have not said so already?

- What thoughts came to you about the other person as your emotions heightened? What were you thinking about yourself? In what ways did these thoughts—about the other person and yourself—heighten your emotional reactions?

- Sometimes when we are in conflict with another person, we perceive that she or he has undermined, challenged, or threatened something or some things that are meaningful to or about us (such as a value, belief, or aspect of our identity). If this applies to you in any way in the specific dispute you are considering here, what did you perceive the other person undermined, challenged, or threatened that contributed to your heightened emotions? What did you most need from the other person at the time?

- What would you like to have said or done differently in this conflict if you had it to do over again? What would be different between you and the other person if you responded the way you describe here? What do your answers here say about the reasons for your heightened emotions, if applicable?

- What is clearer to you now about understanding your emotions in that conflict than when you started this series of questions? From what you have learned here about what heightens emotions during conflict, what, if anything, do you now also understand about the other person's heightened emotions in the dispute that you had not considered?

- Going forward, how do you want to respond that reflects how you would prefer to interact the next time someone provokes you? What will help you in your future conflicts to regulate your emotions if they begin to heighten? What understanding of your emotions do you have now that will help you in future conflicts?

- What else occurs to you as you consider these questions?

- What insights do you have?

Getting Revved Up

As with **Understanding Heightened Emotions When in Conflict** (just discussed), what often happens in the middle of an interpersonal dispute is that, for various reasons, one or both people become increasingly agitated. Words and emotions accelerate in intensity and negativity at these times. This may show up in a number of other ways too, such as yelling (discussed in the topic **Yelling When in Conflict**, later in this chapter) and becoming more aggressive, critical, and blameful. The outpouring of feelings from the faucet of vitriol that frequently opens up at these times may also lead to an exaggeration of everything related to the conflict. It is a time during which we commonly feel out of control and out of choice.

"Revving up" is an expression that describes such a dynamic, which sometimes happens for one or both people during a conflict. The phrase is often associated with accelerating the speed of a car or other vehicle. One resource, however, describes "getting revved up" as when things become "more productive."[6] This definition may apply to the notion of positive conflict—such as when we become actively and constructively engaged in a discussion—aiming to reconcile differences and put our collective energy into finding a mutually satisfactory outcome.

The next set of questions is for people who "rev up" in the middle of a conflict in not-so-positive ways—sometimes for no apparent reason—and who would prefer to regulate their emotions. One way of examining how *not* to rev up is to picture ourselves at a crossroads as soon as we sense our emotions accelerating. At the crossroads we have a choice about which route to take, including one that is conflict-masterful and consistent with how we prefer to be and be seen. (The concept of choice in conflict is also discussed in Chapter 2 in the topic **The Platinum Moment of Choice in Conflict** and later in this chapter under **Choices About Responding When in Conflict**.)

QUESTIONS

- When you consider one conflict during which you revved up, what did you specifically say or do that constitutes "revving up"?

- What else accelerated for you as you revved up—such as your voice, heart rate, and so on—if you consider factors other than those you referred to in the first question?

- Which specific emotions accelerated?

- What motivated you to rev up?

- In what ways did the other person rev up too? What seemed to motivate that for her or him? What might you have said or done that contributed to her or his revving up?

- What choices did you have about what to say or do to decelerate things? Which choice might have been most suitable? Why is that so?

- At what point might you have exercised that choice (your answer to the previous question)? What specifically would you have said or done?

- What self-talk might you engage in to help regulate your emotions when you begin to rev up? How else might you regulate your emotions?

- If you do not want to rev up next time you are in conflict, what conflict-masterful approaches might you take in your responses to the other person? What will be especially different in the ways you respond with those approaches? What difference do you expect those ways will make to the interaction and outcome of the conflict?

- If you want to rev things up in a positive way during your next conflict, what other conflict-masterful approaches might you choose?

- What else occurs to you as you consider these questions?

- What insights do you have?

Body and Facial Language of Conflict

Often, in the aftermath of conflict, we may recall a scowl on the other person's face, or maybe it is her or his overbearing or threatening demeanor that stays with us. Eye-rolling, grimaces, sneering, and turning away from us may be things we remember. It may instead be a look of hurt, despair, and surrender that affects us. Or, a placating or imploring façade may stand out in our mind's eye.

We may wonder if such appearances are purposeful posturing techniques to manipulate us, or meaningful messages about the other person's state of mind and heart. Or, are they signals we find ambiguous and difficult to decipher? During conflicts, our ability to read body and facial language is often diminished, and this adds to our feelings of vulnerability and insecurity.

During conflict there are times when we, too, likely come across in ways that are off-putting or that confuse the other person. We are not necessarily conscious of how our faces appear, or how our bodies are otherwise "talking." What we are saying may not be consistent with our words and actions. If we lose perspective on the situation, we may also lose our awareness about how we are contributing to the other person's tension with our facial and body language. We might, however, be intentional about how we come across—fully aware that our body and facial language are off-putting and even threatening, daunting, and confusing for her or him.

At times of conflict, the only mirror in front of us is the other person, who often reflects our reactions, our physical mannerisms, and our language, and vice versa. In an effort to build conflict mastery, then, it is important not only to be conscious of how we are coming across during a conflict. It also helps to notice the other person's facial and body language, and consider what seems dissonant, challenging, threatening, and so on. Sometimes the language we are "speaking" to each another at these times tells us more than words do, and has a huge impact on the interrelational dynamic and the course the conflict takes.

One suggestion is to ask for a "time-out" as soon as we experience and observe negative facial and body language in the middle of a heated discussion. If we remove ourselves from the interaction temporarily and process what seems to be happening for us and the other person, we are more likely to gain emotional distance and also increase our awareness of how our facial and body language may be contributing to the discord. We may also obtain a better read on the other person or, at least, open the dialogue to understand what she or he is experiencing.

The following questions are meant to hold up a mirror to examine how your facial and body language may negatively contribute to conflict situations and your quest for conflict mastery.

(In Chapter 2, several topics also discussed somatic signs—such as **The Cold Shoulder**, **Chip on the Shoulder**, and **That Put My Back Up**—and may be helpful to review here. What these idioms represent, discussed in Chapter 2: Before Conflict, may, like other aspects of body and facial language, be evident during or after conflict, too. **Getting Your Nose Out of Joint**, later in this chapter, deals with another somatic sign of conflict. In Chapter 4: After Conflict, the topic **Observing Ourselves Through Someone Else's Eyes** also speaks to this subject.)

QUESTIONS

- In general, what are you conscious of about your body language that negatively affects your conflictual interactions? What do you know happens to your face that does not help? What else, if anything, have others told you about how your body and face appear when you are in conflict that they consider counterproductive?

- What sorts of behaviors, attitudes, words, and so on of others commonly result in your reacting with the facial and somatic reactions you just described?

- When you consider a specific conflict in which you know your face and body language had a negative effect, to what, specifically, were you reacting? In what specific ways did your body and face demonstrate your reaction in that situation?

- What message or messages were you meaning to convey by reacting the way you describe (your answer to the previous question)? How do you think the other person interpreted the message(s) that was consistent with your intentions? What may she or he have misinterpreted or *not* understood?

- Which of your facial or body language messages do you think were least productive in that conflict interaction? Which were most productive?

- What would you have said if you had conveyed your message(s) in words instead?

- In general, what do other people do with their faces and bodies that you find offensive, unsettling, and so on when you are in conflict with them? What is it specifically about those mannerisms that is most off-putting? What words might you use (rather than those here—offensive, unsettling, and off-putting) to describe your experience of others' faces and bodies that negatively affects you during conflict?

- In a specific conflict situation in which the other person demonstrated body or facial language that provoked you, what specifically did she or he do? How did you interpret the message(s) conveyed? In what ways did you mirror back some or all of these same facial or body mannerisms (your answer to the first part of this question)?

- If you chose positive body and facial language to respond instead in that situation, what would that look like? In what different ways might the other person interact in response to your positive demeanor?

- When you are in the middle of conflict, what might you do to restrain yourself from using facial and body language that you know is not productive, appropriate, and useful? What might you do to refrain from mirroring the other person's negative facial and body language?

• What else occurs to you as you consider these questions?

• What insights do you have?

Fears About Tears

When some of us get upset, we cry. It's just what happens. Crying is considered by some to be gender- and sometimes culture-specific. However, the reality is that both men and women from all cultures shed tears for many reasons and in many contexts, including when experiencing strong emotions during interpersonal conflict. Both genders also weep internally, though those words are not necessarily used to describe this phenomenon.

"Internal weeping" refers to what happens when we experience deep and overwhelming feelings about the situation or the other person, and words to express them do not come easily. We may not want to vocalize our pain, or we struggle to articulate the words that describe what is happening for us. Internal weeping may include a sense of helplessness, despair, sadness, and other emotions, some of which can be immobilizing. Persons who do not cry outwardly may cry inwardly. Even those who cry externally may weep inside.

For those of us who cry outwardly, doing so provides, among other things, a release of built-up emotions, including hurt, anger, frustration, disappointment, and so on. Some feel embarrassed about crying, though, and fear it is perceived as manipulative or dramatic, or as a sign of weakness or being out of control.

Further, worrying about crying when engaging in a conflict and being judged for doing so often results in fears about making *any* effort to communicate. It may mean holding back and not fully expressing ourselves—resulting in avoidance, giving in, or compromising something that we do not want to compromise.

Those who do not typically demonstrate emotions with tears when in conflict, and those who are generally put off by them, may view the person who cries in the ways mentioned above. Fears about tears may also result in feelings of helplessness, guilt, and confusion about what to say in response and how to manage our reactions. For some, tears halt communication altogether, and the fear then becomes whether there will be a way to resolve, or at least discuss, the pertinent issues, their impact, and how to move forward.

The questions on this topic will resonate for readers who fear tears or have other negative emotions about other people crying during a conflict. On this subject, **Fears About Being in Conflict**—a topic later in this chapter—and Chapter 1 provide further reasons for fears that lead to tears.

QUESTIONS

- In general, what do you fear about people who cry when you are in conflict with them? How else do you describe the impact on you at these times? What is it about tears that you find most off-putting, disturbing, concerning, and so on? What three other words would you use to describe the impact besides those here (off-putting, disturbing, concerning)?

- When you consider a specific conflict situation in which the other person's tears had an adverse impact on you, how would you describe the specific effect they had on you? What emotions do you think she or he was experiencing?

- What do you know or think the other person was crying about in that situation? What do you *not* know for certain about the reasons for her or his tears? What messages did you perceive the other person was conveying to you by crying at that time?

- What fears did you experience about the other person's tears in that situation? How realistic were the fears, scaling them from 1 to 5—5 being "absolutely realistic" and 1 being "absolutely unrealistic"? How does your rating influence your hopes about the outcome of this conflict? What else does your rating mean as compared to a higher number? As compared to a lower number?

- How did you respond to the other person's tears, if you did, that indicated you felt fearful (or another reaction, if you can name one)? How did you react in your body and face that may have demonstrated your fears (or other reaction, if you can name it)? How did you react inwardly? If you were weeping internally, what were you experiencing?

- Which of your reactions to the other person's tears helped things? In what ways? Which did *not* help? In what ways?

- From your perspective, how are the other person's tears influencing the outcome? If the conflict is over, how did the tears influence the outcome?

- What conflict-masterful approaches have you observed or used that work effectively when the other person cries during a conflict? If you have cried during a conflict, what has the other person said or done that was effective? What makes the various approaches you just referred to effective?

- How would things have been different in the situation you consider here if you had handled the other person's tears in one or more of the ways you described as effective in the previous question? Which specific way is most likely to make that difference (or those differences)?

- What do you want to fear less from now on when it comes to other people's tears when you are in conflict with them? How will you accomplish that?

- What else occurs to you as you consider these questions?

- What insights do you have?

Yelling When in Conflict

During conflict, some of us yell for various reasons. Yelling might be an outlet for built-up frustrations and other emotions we are experiencing. It might reflect an effort to win a fight, to make a point, or to reject someone or an idea. It might be to assert power, to put down the other person, or to defend our views. Maybe other ways of expressing what is important to us, and what we are feeling, are not working. We may also yell when the emotional pain we are experiencing is so deep that shouting seems like the only way of coping. Whatever the reason, for some of us, conflict causes sounds and words to fly from our mouths loudly and aggressively. And we cannot take back the fact that we yelled, or what we said.

More often than not, yelling—whatever motivates it—serves to heighten the tension, discord, and emotions, and the interaction deteriorates when this occurs. Whether or not the other person yells back, the issues in dispute easily get lost amid the noise that shouting creates. The conflict often becomes more personal, and the flood of feelings drowns out other things that matter—including the crux of the controversy and what is important about it for us—individually and collectively.

The following series of questions invites people who tend to yell, or have yelled during a conflict, to explore this topic and increase your conflict mastery in this regard. These questions also help when considering what compels someone to yell at you during conflict, if that has occurred. Other previous topics in this chapter about emotions are relevant here, such as **Understanding Heightened Emotions When in Conflict**, **Getting Revved Up**, **Fears About Being in Conflict**, and **The Conflict Groan** (next topic).

QUESTIONS

- In general, under what sorts of circumstances have you yelled at another person in a conflict? When you consider a specific situation, what happened that resulted in your yelling? What did you yell?

- What message(s) were you trying to convey? What were you hoping might happen when you yelled?

- What impact did you observe or hear from the other person when you yelled?

- What message(s) do you think she or he got from what you yelled? How did yelling help the situation? How did it *not* help?

- How did it feel to yell? What were you feeling at the time about the other person? What were you feeling about yourself?

- When someone has yelled at you during a conflict, what seemed to motivate her or him to do so? What message(s) do you think she or he was trying to convey? What message(s) did you hear?

- What do you think the other person was hoping might happen by yelling at you in that scenario? What did happen?

- How did you feel about yourself in that same scenario—when the other person yelled at you? What was your impression of the other person at that time?

- If you think about it now, how might you best respond, in a conflict-masterful way, to someone else yelling at you if that happens in the future?

- Going forward, in what conflict-masterful ways might you manage situations yourself—instead of yelling?

- What else occurs to you as you consider these questions?

- What insights do you have?

The Conflict Groan

Conflict groans essentially refer to the internal emotional reactions we experience in our hearts, minds, and bodies to things that upset us, and that topple our sense of well-being during interpersonal conflicts. Groans may take the form of grunts, deep sighs, and other sounds that are not words but which form a language all their own.

Some of us purposely try to suppress groans. We may try, too, to convince ourselves that they do not really matter, or we reckon they will just go away. At times, though, our internal groans may become so loud in our heads that they are like yells, and the noise interferes with our ability to hear ourselves or what the other person is saying and meaning.

Sometimes groans seep out when we can no longer contain our inner voice from outwardly expressing our frustration or other emotions. As with internal weeping (see **Fears About Tears**, earlier in this chapter), we may groan because we do not want to vocalize our feelings, or perhaps we are struggling to articulate what we are experiencing. Or, maybe our fears are prevailing, and we are reticent to share what is on our mind. (See also **Fears About Being in Conflict**, later in this chapter.)

Whether we groan internally or externally, our balance usually gets shaky when we experience the emotions that lead to a groan. More things may arise, too, that affect the relationship dynamic. For instance, we may begin to build a case against the other person. Or, we look for things to justify and support our views, and generally lose perspective on what the conflict is about and our part in it.

Lots of things occur during the course of a dispute that raise an internal or external groan in us. If we pinpoint the specific drivers, we are usually better able to understand how they contribute to our interactions. For instance, we hear a truth we hate to face; we observe a look or attitude that is off-putting; we disapprove of the other person's perspective that is diametrically opposed to ours or that we find hurtful, mean, infuriating, or offensive; we say something we immediately regret; or we feel an overwhelm of despair or other deep emotions. **Understanding Heightened Emotions When in Conflict**, earlier in this chapter, also discusses things that stimulate reactions in us during conflict.

Such reasons for our groans, and others, are important clues to consider in our efforts to obtain a stronger grasp on what the conflict dynamic is about. Identifying the reasons for our groans also inherently provides us with ideas for addressing them rather than struggling with what they feel like inside us—even if we externalize them. In turn, this helps us to learn and build conflict-masterful ways to respond to words and actions that stimulate our groans.

By looking back on a certain dispute in which you groaned internally (or externally), your answers to the next set of questions may help you better understand what brought on the groan and the impact it had on you and the conflict. Your answers will also enable you to pay attention to what the groan represents—as an early sign to consider so that your choices about how to proceed preempt unnecessary internal and external conflict.

QUESTIONS

- What were you reacting to that brought on an internal or external groan? Which was it—internal or external?

- What three words describe what you were experiencing?

- What did your internal groan sound like? If it became external, what did it sound like?

- At what point in the interaction did you first become aware that a groan was beginning to erupt? What was happening at the time that stimulated a reaction in you?

- What were you thinking at the time you experienced the groan? What were you feeling?

- What did your body and face do, if anything, when you experienced the groan internally or when it erupted externally, such that the other person was likely aware that you were reacting to something?

- If the other person could hear your groan, what did she or he likely hear contained in it? What might someone who knows you well hear in your groan that the other person might miss?

- How did your groan change the interaction for the better? In what way(s) did it negatively influence the situation?

- When you consider that dispute now, if a groan still remains inside you about it, why is that the case? If you want to get rid of the groan, how might you do so?

- Generally speaking, what do you think groans represent when you internally feel them? What do they mean when you externalize them?

- When you think about this now, if groans are clues, what do they signal for you? In what conflict-masterful ways might you effectively process them in the future when they begin to erupt? What do you expect will be different in your interactions if you use that approach?

- What else occurs to you as you consider these questions?

- What insights do you have?

Getting Your Nose Out of Joint

Idioms about conflict provide interesting ways to understand and reframe our interactions. Giving idioms meaning according to our individual interpretations helps us reappraise the situation, the other person, and ourselves. Getting our "nose out of joint" is one such phrase that refers to a reaction to conflict, and its meaning—developed in this topic—provides a way to explore a response you may have experienced or observed.

The origin of the phrase "getting your nose out of joint" dates back to 1581 and was reportedly used by Barnaby Rich in *His Farewell to Militarie Profession*: "It could bee no other then his owne manne, that has thrust his nose so farre out of ioynte [*sic*]."[7] This meaning and others referred to more currently reflect a physical sense of resentment, hurt feelings, and upset in response to an offence.[8] Such a reaction may arise visibly, for instance, when we show defensive reactions to the other person's getting her or his way in a conflict, or when she or he offends us with words and actions, or otherwise provokes us. (**Chip on the Shoulder** and **The Cold Shoulder**, described in Chapter 2, are two similar idioms.)

Having a "nose out of joint" conjures up a vivid image—of a nose broken, crooked, contorted, and imbalanced (literally and figuratively). Just thinking of someone who actually has her or his nose out of joint makes for a painful picture. We can only imagine what it feels like, including the pain. Applying the metaphor to conflict, we may also interpret the image as reflecting deep feelings of hurt, anger, disappointment, betrayal, injustice, and sadness.

As with many other reactions, getting a nose out of joint may be evident before, during, or after a conflict. The topic is included in this chapter because the experience is common during conflict. The questions here, which pertain to the immediate experience of feeling your nose is out of joint, might also be asked using different verb tenses in relation to interactions before and after conflict. (This is also the case with other topics and questions.)

If you feel, or someone has suggested, that you appear to have your nose out of joint during a present or past conflict, this topic will be of special interest to you. (The questions may work even if the exact idiom does not resonate, but the meaning does.) Bringing to mind a specific conflict will help you answer the following questions.

QUESTIONS

- How do you describe what the phrase "nose out of joint" means as it applies to your reaction in a specific dispute?

- How does it feel to have your nose out of joint?

- How might you describe your physical appearance (such as your body and face) in this circumstance?

- How else might the image of having your nose out of joint be described by some-one observing you? When you have seen others and could say their nose was out of joint, how would you describe what that looks like? What is the impact on you when you observe others with their nose out of joint?

- At what particular point did your nose become disjointed in the dispute you referred to in the first question, above (for example, what did the other person specifically say or do)?

- What could the other person have said or done differently so that your nose would not have become disjointed?

- What could you have said or done differently to prevent your nose from becoming disjointed?

- What could you say or do now to put your nose back into place? How will your interaction with the other person be different once your nose is no longer out of joint?

- How do you expect to feel about yourself when your nose is back in place? How do you expect to feel about the other person?

- In what ways, if any, have you reappraised the conflict situation by answering these questions? How have you reappraised the other person, if you have? How have you reappraised yourself, if that is the case?

- What else occurs to you as you consider these questions?

- What insights do you have?

Two Sides to the Story

When we are in conflict, we are not always able to articulate what is unfolding for us. What we are reacting to, what we are thinking, what we are attributing to the other person, and so on are often exaggerated, confused, or clouded by our emotional experience of the situation. To an even greater degree, we are unlikely to have a full sense of where the other person is coming from. We see the other person's perspective through a lens that is foggy with our own viewpoints, feelings, and vulnerabilities.

Acknowledging mutuality in conflict, a significant dimension of conflict intelligence, refers to the ability not only to gain a clear understanding about our own perspective on a matter; it also means gaining an understanding of where the other person is coming from, to whatever extent possible. This is of the nature of the often-used expression "walking a mile in someone's shoes,"[9] which suggests, too, that we gain empathy for others when we do so.

You will have read about of the principle of mutuality in Chapter 1 and in topics from other chapters that ask you to reflect on the shared responsibility of being in conflict, such as **The Platinum Moment of Choice in Conflict** in Chapter 2, and **The Conflict Iceberg** and **Positions and Interests** in this chapter.

Contemplating two sides of our conflict stories when they start to evolve—and before initiating a discussion or responding to the other person—helps us gain distance, a concept also explored in the topic **Understanding Heightened Emotions When in Conflict**, in this chapter, and **Gaining Distance from Hurts**, in Chapter 4. Among other things, gaining emotional and cognitive distance enables us to calm our emotions, broaden our perspectives, and ultimately respond in more constructive ways than we may otherwise do if we remain focused only on what we want and are experiencing.

When we consider a fuller picture of the dynamic, we are more likely, too, to make the sort of connection between ourselves and the other person that facilitates hearing and understanding—and being heard and understood—and that builds empathy. The following questions further help to develop mutuality in the midst of conflict.

QUESTIONS

- When you consider a specific dispute, what is your side of the story? How might the other person describe her or his side of the story?

- What might be a third side of the story? For instance, if an objective person observed and heard the two of you during your conflict, what might be her or his perception of what is going on between you that is different from these versions (your answers to the previous question)?

- What do you think you and the other person most disagree on? What would the other person say you most disagree on? How would you describe what you both likely agree on?

- What did you expect from the other person regarding the conflict? What do you think the other person expected from you?

- What do you *not* know or understand about the other person's perspective on this situation? What does the other person *not* seem to know or understand about yours?

- If applicable, what happened that got in your way of being able to hear and understand the other person's perspective during the conflict? What might be standing, or have stood, in her or his way of being able to hear and understand your perspective? (For example, consider, when answering both questions, the way you were communicating with each other, what you two were saying or doing, and so on.)

- What is most important to you about the conflict? What do you think might be most important to the other person?

- If you were to re-script the story of what occurred between you to have a positive ending, what would it sound like? How might the other person want to re-script the story to have a positive ending? What, if anything, do you two have in common here?

- What might be a mutually satisfactory ending? What conflict-masterful approaches would help make the conflict end that way—if you want it to?

- If a mutually satisfactory resolution does not seem feasible, how might the conflict still have a positive outcome? What conflict-masterful approaches would facilitate that?

- What else occurs to you as you consider these questions?

- What insights do you have?

Agreeing to Disagree

Many of us think we have to "win" disagreements. In the midst of a conflict, this typically translates into expecting the other person to concede to our viewpoints and the outcome we want. The competitive underpinnings of this approach set up a win–lose scenario. Not only does it not reconcile our differences; such an approach precludes an opportunity to engage in a more expansive conversation aimed at reaching an outcome that is mutually satisfactory, and that does not threaten the relationship.

Another possible outcome is to agree to disagree. That is, the conflict may result in no resolution. However, even if that is the case, sharing our disparate views in non-threatening and non-competitive ways opens up settlement possibilities and, at least, facilitates a discussion in which we both hear and are heard. Though the idea of agreeing to disagree does not always resonate for everyone as a way to reconcile the relationship or the issues in dispute, this topic considers that it is one possible option.

To check out the notion of agreeing to disagree, it helps, first, to consider that there is potential to come to an agreement once we have a full grasp of the situation. This means—to begin with—sharing our different perspectives about a specific situation, as with **Two Sides to the Story** (the previous topic). Sharing, too, what is most important to each of us is also a major part of this effort. Once we have engaged in these steps, it then helps to consider common ground and what we might mutually agree on. Comparing what possible outcomes may work for us both—rather than operating on the basis that it has to be only one or the other's desired result—further expands the discussion to see whether we may discover a resolution that we both support.

The above exercise essentially filters through many aspects of the conflict dynamic to be able to contemplate what may be workable solutions for us and the other person. Once we have done so, if no agreement seems to be possible, the choice remains to maintain our opposing views and consider how to move forward regardless. Ultimately, then, agreement depends in large part on what is important to us, what options may be mutually acceptable, or whether maintaining our initial expectations—without resolution—is an outcome we are prepared to live with.

The following questions provide a self-reflective way of approaching conflict scenarios when agreement does not seem to be forthcoming. Since agreeing to disagree is one option, processing that possibility is included and is part of weighing all options. **Two Sides to the Story** and **Positions and Interests**, both in this chapter, also explore a number of aspects of the concepts discussed here.

QUESTIONS

- When you consider a specific ongoing disagreement, what is your perspective about the matters that are in dispute? How might the other person answer this question?

- What part of the other person's views on what is happening are most similar to yours? What parts are most different from yours?

- What do you think an optimal outcome might be? Why is that so? What might the other person consider the optimal outcome? Why is that so?

- What other possible solution(s) might there be, whether or not you like it (them)? Which of these, if any, might you be willing to accept as you think about it now? Which might be acceptable to the other person?

- What, of all solutions you put forth so far, or variations of them, might you both accept?

- If the answer to the previous question is "none," what downsides are there for your going forward without agreement? What might be the downsides for the other person?

- If the notion of agreeing to disagree does not work for you, what are your options going forward? What are the advantages of those options for you? What are the disadvantages for you? What are the advantages of these options for the other person? What are the disadvantages for her or him? What, if anything, do your answers here open up for you?

- If, after your analysis here, you discover that a mutually acceptable solution is not likely, how might that be a positive outcome for you anyway? How might it be positive for the other person?

- What other positive results might emerge from having explored the possibilities, even if you agree to disagree?

- Even if you prefer to reach agreement—but an agreement is not forthcoming— how might you reconcile this outcome in a conflict-masterful way and move on?

- What else occurs to you as you consider these questions?

- What insights do you have?

Choices About Responding When in Conflict

There are times during an interpersonal conflict when we are highly reactive. Though we are conscious that some strategies for coping with the conflict dynamic are not constructive, we may rely on habitual yet unproductive ways of communicating—feeling upset and at a loss to know what else to do. In these cases, we may strongly assert viewpoints in an effort to be heard. We may try to shut down the other person. We may blame, call names, yell, curse, criticize, or use guilt and other techniques to hurt her or him. We may walk away.

Besides the conflict itself, fatigue, personal or professional worries, and other stressors contribute to how reactive we are and for what reason. When something said or done triggers deep emotions, there is added strain, and these feelings sometimes take over such that we find ourselves responding in extreme ways. We may also interact uncharacteristically with other people in our lives owing to the lack of balance and harmony we are experiencing as a result of the interpersonal conflict.

While it is challenging to distance ourselves in the heat of the moment to be able to figure out what is happening, this is an important competency to learn in the development of conflict mastery. Otherwise, the situation is likely to turn into an unnecessary conflict, and even when it is ostensibly over, our feelings of shame, vulnerability, sadness, and upset may linger indefinitely. (See also the topics **Understanding Heightened Emotions When in Conflict** and **Two Sides to the Story**, earlier in this chapter.)

Although it may not feel like it, we have choices along the entire conflict trajectory, including during it. That is, despite time-worn habits that we are inclined to rely on, we have choices that represent other, more conflict-masterful ways of responding. (See also the topics **The Platinum Moment of Choice in Conflict** and **Our Conflict Habits**, in Chapter 2.) If we want to learn how to be in conflict differently, it helps to consider our options and practice new and different ways to respond and communicate more constructively during conflict.

The suggested starting point is to acknowledge that we not only have choices. We also have within us the wisdom, ability, knowledge, and courage to select responses that align with our values and intentions, and with how we want to be and be perceived. Here are some questions to inspire thinking about choices and different ways of responding during conflict.

QUESTIONS

- How would you describe one or more ways you habitually react in a conflict when you are upset that you would like to change?

- Besides what you have just answered, what else, if anything, have you been told, directly or indirectly, by friends, family, colleagues, co-workers, and others about ways you habitually react—to your detriment—during conflict?

- What is motivating you at this point to change one or more of your habits about how you interact during conflict? Which habit will you start with?

- During a specific dispute, how was that habit (your answer to the previous question) counterproductive?

- In that same dispute, what choices did you have about what you said or did that would have been better aligned with how you prefer to interact? Which of your intentions are reflected in those choices?

- What ways of responding to conflict do you admire in others that are pertinent and would have presented other possible choices?

- What stopped you from interacting according to one or more of the other choices you had (your answers to the previous two questions)?

- When you gain increased conflict mastery, it is likely you will be, and be perceived, differently. What do you want people you respect to say about the choices you make in responding during conflict that is different from what they may now say about how you respond? (Consider, for instance, your answer to the second question in this set.) How else do you want to be perceived regarding how you respond when in conflict? Which of your values are encompassed in your answers to these two questions?

- In general, what positive attributes do you know you have that indicate your current capability to transform your counterproductive reactions to conflict into constructive responses? What else do you want or need to work on to be more skilled at the changes you wish to make?

- Going forward, how will you choose which conflict-masterful responses to use during conflict?

- What else occurs to you as you consider these questions?

- What insights do you have?

Positions and Interests

In the field of alternative dispute resolution, one of the roles of mediators is to help people in dispute work together to reconcile their differences and reach a mutually acceptable resolution about issues they do not agree on. As in **Agreeing to Disagree** (earlier in this chapter), when people hold disparate perspectives on issues and what happened between them, they usually disagree on what constitutes an appropriate settlement, too.

By the time the disputants talk the matter through in the mediation process, they have often become entrenched in their positions and the relationship is suffering. In the end, the parties may resolve matters in mutually acceptable ways (or settle in ways that do not fully satisfy them), or they may agree to disagree in that forum. This topic discusses the concepts of positions and interests, and what they mean in the context of trying to settle issues in dispute.

Positions reflect what we assert as our perspective and what we want as an outcome. The more we defend our positions, the stronger we seem to hold onto them. It also seems our identity and ego become attached to what we perceive as the rightness of our views—and we defend them at every turn. Along the way, growing emotions often impair our reasoning and problem-solving skills, precluding collaborative and conciliatory communications. The topic **Making Others Wrong**, earlier in this chapter, also speaks to the same dynamics.

Interests, on the other hand, reflect not only what is important to us as an outcome. They also reflect the reasons they are important. As in **The Conflict Iceberg** (at the beginning of this chapter), interests lie beneath what we say we want—and they reveal our hopes, needs, values, beliefs, and expectations. Unfortunately, these things frequently become obfuscated in the fight for our positions. The core of the disagreement often gets lost at these times, too, and ideas about what makes for a mutually acceptable resolution are not easily forthcoming.

To identify common ground, if there is any, and reach solutions that work for both parties when in conflict (if that is what is wanted), it helps to consider our interests by articulating what is important to us and why. Doing so tends to open up the possibilities for resolution that are otherwise limited by intractable positions. **Agreeing to Disagree** and **Two Sides to the Story**, earlier in this chapter, also address these concepts.

This series of questions is designed to help you analyze the concept of positions and interests in a specific dispute. **"Thinking Outside the Box" When in Conflict** (the next topic) expands on efforts to seek solution.

QUESTIONS

- What are the issues in dispute in the conflict you have in mind—from your perspective? What would the other person identify as the issues in dispute from her or his perspective? What else is the conflict about?

- What would you say you both agree on right now? What other common ground might you and the other person share?

- What is your position on what constitutes the optimal solution? Why is that solution important to you—including what your interests are, as described in the introduction to this topic (fourth paragraph, above)?

- What is the other person's position on what constitutes the best solution, as far as you know? Why is that solution important to her or him—including what her or his interests may be?

- What other options might there be for resolution, or variations of those you have already considered?

- What are the advantages for you of each of the options you identified in the previous question, including the ones you and the other person began with? What are the advantages of each for her or him? What are the disadvantages for you of each of the options, including the ones you and the other person began with? What are the disadvantages of each for her or him?

- If you are realizing that matters may not settle in a mutually satisfactory way, what does that mean for you? What does it mean for the relationship? In what conflict-masterful ways will you proceed if things do not settle?

- If you see there are mutually acceptable solutions that might be possible, what are they? On a scale of 1 to 5, 5 being "very much" and 1 being "not at all," how would you rate your willingness to accept the mutually agreeable solutions you identified here? If your rating is lower than 5, what does that mean?

- If you wish to proceed and present the mutually acceptable solutions, as you identified them in the previous question, to the other person, what conflict-masterful ways will you use to do so?

- What will you take away as learning from answering the questions in this topic—whether or not things settle between you?

- What else occurs to you as you consider these questions?

- What insights do you have?

"Thinking Outside the Box" When in Conflict

The expression "thinking outside the box" typically refers to being creative about ideas that lie beyond the parameters of our usual way of thinking and being. When this concept comes up in the conflict management context, it usually refers to contemplating the various settlement options available to the people in dispute in view of their opposing positions. Specifically, the "outside the box" notion urges disputants to get away from constrained thinking about solutions, and engage in more expansive discussions that consider the range of possibilities that may be mutually acceptable.

Because emotional reactions often prevail in the middle of a dispute, and our ability to be creative becomes increasingly limited the more upset we become, giving ourselves time to think out conflict-related matters and how to resolve them is crucial. One way of becoming more attuned to ourselves and the other person—to increase the ability to think broader and deeper—is, literally and figuratively, to stand back from the fray that adversely affects our hearts and brains. Doing so opens up the space surrounding them and also strengthens the ability to tap into our inner resources and reframe the conflict. This, in turn, helps us think outside our usual frames of reference and discover different possibilities that would not otherwise emerge at these times.

To engage in "outside the box" thinking requires not only a clear head, including emotional and cognitive readiness; it also requires the willingness to acknowledge the other person's perspective, and to consider a range of possible options that may be mutually satisfactory. In addition, being creative requires us to step outside our comfort zone, particularly if we feel strongly about our viewpoint and getting our way. If we want to reconcile the matters in dispute, being innovative about ways to move forward is critical.

Here are some questions that support efforts to "think outside the box" during conflict. Previous topics in this chapter—**Positions and Interests, Two Sides to the Story**, and **Agreeing to Disagree**—are also relevant and helpful in this exercise to facilitate the process of thinking more creatively.

QUESTIONS

- When you consider a specific dispute, what is it about? What solution do you want? What solution does the other person want?

- How would you rate the importance to you of resolving this dispute in a mutually satisfactory way on a scale of 1 to 5, 5 being "extremely" and 1 being "not at all"? If your answer is 5, what "outside the box" resolution options exist (that neither you nor the other person has put forward yet) that might be mutually satisfactory?

- What might a respected mentor, friend, or colleague suggest as other possible solutions that are even more "outside the box" and might also be mutually satisfactory? What other mutually acceptable possibilities would you suggest to a close friend in a similar situation? What is the most "outside the box" solution that occurs to you?

- If you are finding it difficult to "think outside the box," what obstacles are preventing you from finding new and creative solutions that might meet both of your needs?

- What needs to happen for you to remove any obstacles that might be keeping you from thinking broader and deeper about options to resolve your dispute? What other options might emerge when you contemplate removing the obstacles you identified?

- Which part(s) of the possible solutions described so far would you be willing to consider (and be comfortable doing so) to reach a mutually satisfactory solution? Which part(s) of the possible solutions do you think the other person might accept?

- When you consider all your answers so far, what variations of all the options may be creative and mutually acceptable?

- If you chose 1 to 4 in the response to the second question in this topic, what does that rating mean regarding this conflict and your answers so far?

- If you conclude that you will not be able to live with a resolution that does not fully satisfy you, what does that determination mean going forward?

- What learning have you gained from "thinking outside the box" in this set of questions, whether or not a mutually acceptable solution is apparent?

- What else occurs to you as you consider these questions?

- What insights do you have?

"Settle Down"

Some phrases that may be directed by one of the people to the other during conflict—such as "settle down," "just calm yourself," and "you don't need to get upset"—can actually lead to increased defensiveness and other negative reactions, even when they are well intentioned. Hushing hand gestures result in similar responses, because such actions are typically experienced as dismissive and undermining. Those on the receiving end perceive and resent that their views and feelings are being quieted, put down, or minimized.

Such statements or physical messages may also be experienced as a power imbalance. That is, the person stating or doing them appears to be dominant or superior and somehow in charge or in control of the situation and the other person. There is even a sense of condescension akin to a parent admonishing a child, or a teacher shushing a student.

Why do we use these tactics? Underlying reasons may include a fear of the other person's emotions or even our own. We may consider emotions as a sign of weakness or a manipulative ploy. We may sense the other person is purposely derailing the conversation. Maybe we are at a loss about how to have a discussion if things escalate or the conversation goes off topic. Maybe we are becoming more and more anxious ourselves and are projecting our own feelings onto the other person. Perhaps there is some urgency about the conflict's resolution, and we feel frustrated that things are not moving forward. Or, maybe it is a habit learned from experience or observing others trying to calm a person who appears distressed.

Learning to respond to such situations—acknowledging the emotions without shutting down the person or the conversation—is a key part of building conflict mastery. If the other person in your conflict urges you to "settle down" or makes hushing motions, or if you yourself use statements or gestures of this nature, the following questions explore alternative ways of interacting.

QUESTIONS

- When someone communicated a "settle down" statement or gesture that had a negative impact on you during a conflict, what specifically did she or he say or do? What was the impact on you?

- What were you saying or doing that the other person was reacting to by demonstrating "settle down" words or gestures? If you are not sure, what are some possibilities?

- What might the other person not know or understand about why you were reacting at the time she or he tried to shush you?

- What could the other person have said or done instead that would have been more effective for you? What might have precluded her or him from doing that?

- What did you say or do in response to the other person's efforts to calm or quiet you? How did that work? What did you want to say back that you did not? What do you think that might have accomplished if you had? What stopped you?

- What might be other conflict-masterful ways to respond to someone who uses such words or gestures toward you in the future?

- When you think of a specific conflict situation in which you made a statement to the other person such as "settle down" or a hushing gesture, what specifically did you say or do? What motivated you to say or do that?

- How did the other person respond? How was her or his response consistent with what you were hoping to achieve in your efforts to calm or quiet her or him? How was it not consistent?

- What reason or reasons might the other person have given you for her or his reactions (that you tried to calm or quiet)? What difference, if any, would knowing that or those reasons have made?

- When you think about the situation now, what might you say or do in the future that would be more conflict masterful instead of using shushing words or gestures?

- What else occurs to you as you consider these questions?

- What insights do you have?

Getting Unstuck When in Conflict

Sometimes, the more positional we are about an issue or issues in dispute, the more stuck we become about listening to and considering other perspectives. Reconciling matters may seem an unrealistic goal at these times. Our ability to converse and negotiate our differences may increasingly deteriorate as the other person persists with her or his viewpoints in response to us. Or, we may be the one to take a strong stand, and our opposing reaction contributes to and perpetuates the discord. Or, we both are persistent and insistent about our positions.

We get stuck in conflict for many reasons, depending on such variables as the nature of the dispute, who the other person is, how much we want something or to get our way, and the sort of threat we perceive to our values, needs, beliefs, or identity. Other reasons may include overwhelming emotions that choke our ability to express ourselves. Or, we become increasingly confused as tempers flare, and unsure about what we will be able to live with regarding the outcome of the conflict.

A challenging dilemma arises when we're stuck in a conflict. The "stuckness" works both ways, in that it means that neither of us is able to move ahead. Ironically, whether it is one or both parties that get stuck, such a seeming stalemate often represents a crucial turning point in the dispute. Yes, we can agree to disagree, as we have discussed earlier in this chapter. However, if we really want to resolve things in a cooperative way, the "stuckness" is a signal that alerts us to pay close attention to our respective needs to be able to become unstuck and move ahead.

In an attempt to ensure that a turning point such as "stuckness" opens the door rather than closes it, the following set of questions is designed to help unstick things.

QUESTIONS

- When you consider a current conflict in which you are stuck, what is the dispute about? In what ways are you stuck? How might the other person describe how she or he is stuck?

- Can you suggest an image (picture, metaphor) that describes your experience of being stuck?

- What does being stuck mean for you and this conflict? What does it mean for your relationship with the other person?

- What difference does it make to you whether or not you resolve the conflict?

- What would you like to have happen between you two instead of being stuck?

- If you felt you could say anything you want to the other person with no reprisal, what would that be? What does that say about why you are stuck? What does that say about why she or he might be stuck?

- What do you think you need from the other person at this juncture of the conflict? What could the other person say or do that would help you come unstuck? What could you say or do to help yourself come unstuck?

- What do you think the other person needs from you at this time? What, if anything, are you willing to say or do that might help the other person get unstuck—even a little?

- How else might you help the two of you to get unstuck? What settlement possibilities might getting unstuck open up for you both? In what ways might getting unstuck improve your relationship?

- What two words describe what you imagine getting unstuck would feel like?

- What else occurs to you as you consider these questions?

- What insights do you have?

The Elephant in the Room

The "elephant in the room" is a common phrase used when referring to something that has a direct or indirect presence but is not identified or mentioned. Wikipedia defines this concept as "an English metaphorical idiom for an obvious truth that is either being ignored or going unaddressed. ... [It] also applies to an obvious problem or risk no one wants to discuss. It is based on the idea that an elephant in a room would be impossible to overlook; thus, people in the room who pretend the elephant is not there have chosen to avoid dealing with the looming big issue."[10]

When this phrase is applied to interpersonal conflicts, the elephant typically represents an issue the disputing people know is not being acknowledged. "Elephants" may also include unspoken words and feelings. They may be the crux of the conflict and the missing piece of the problem. They may be fears and doubts. They may be a hard truth. Or, they may be the people who have a stake in the outcome yet were not invited to the discussion. In any case, whatever elephants represent, they have a large and all-consuming presence though remaining unidentified.

Some of us try to resolve our conflicts without recognizing the "elephant in the room." Without this acknowledgment, though, the looming idiomatic mammal takes up much space and interferes with productive conflict conversations, reconciliation, and resolution. Because transparency is a key element of constructive conflict communications and lasting settlement, the presence of something that precludes these things from happening requires us to draw on conflict-masterful approaches and face the "elephants" with courage and compassion.

If we do not do so, the elephant that remains unnamed and unaddressed inevitably reappears in subsequent conflicts or shows itself in ways that indicate that the settlement—if one is ostensibly reached—is not solid or durable. That is, the elephant does not go away until it is identified and dealt with. When we are in conflict, we are just as responsible as the other person for inviting the elephant in and paying attention to what it is telling us.

In the quest for conflict mastery on this topic, the following self-reflective questions help to lift the thin veil that somehow hides the huge elephant.

QUESTIONS

- When you consider a current dispute in which an "elephant is in the room," what does the elephant represent that is not being acknowledged or said?

- What do you think has kept the elephant veiled so far?

- If the elephant is identified, what are the risks you are concerned about for yourself? Which of these risks are most realistic? What are the risks for the other person? Which of these risks are most realistic?

- What are the risks for you if the elephant is *not* identified? Which of these risks are most realistic? What may be the risks for the other person if the elephant is *not* identified? Which of these risks are most realistic?

- In addition to the risks you referred to in the last two questions, what other considerations have an impact on whether to identify the elephant in the room?

- What else, if anything, is affected by the unaddressed elephant regarding the conflict between you and the other person that you have not mentioned? Who else is affected?

- How is the unspoken and unacknowledged elephant currently affecting your relationship with the other person? How is it affecting resolution of the issue(s) in dispute?

- If you have not already answered the following questions, in what specific ways would bringing the elephant into the conversation change things for you for the better? For the other person? In what specific ways might identifying the elephant in the room help the relationship for the better?

- If you think it is important to identify the elephant—regardless of which of you does so—what do you want to be most prepared for?

- How might you bring the elephant into the room, if you choose to do so, in a conflict-masterful way—despite the possible risks? Besides courage and compassion, what else do you need to make this happen, if you proceed?

- What else occurs to you as you consider these questions?

- What insights do you have?

Fears About Being in Conflict

Sometimes during conflict we lose our confidence and composure. We may become plagued with self-doubt and feel we are not able to stand up for ourselves. We may back down at these times and give in to the other person. We may admonish ourselves for lack of courage or "guts." These sorts of regrets and self-limiting beliefs eat away at our self-esteem and confidence, and as a consequence, we may feel all the more helpless and powerless during a conflict. Though not always expressed, such variables often cause us to experience a range of fears about the dynamic evolving between us and the other person.

As discussed in Chapter 1, fear of the unknown commonly prevails during conflict. Fears may arise over whether the issues in dispute will be resolved and whether our relationship will survive. Or, we may fear the loss of face, reputation, security, control, and so on.

Other fears—such as being hurt, alienated, embarrassed, shamed, rejected, and of hurting the other person—may arise. We may experience fears because we see the other person as more powerful or even more vulnerable, and we are ambivalent about how or whether to continue to push or defend our views. We may fear tears—ours and the other person's—as discussed in **Fears About Tears**, earlier in this chapter.

When we become fearful, we typically lose energy and feel broken. We may experience ongoing stress and anxiety that have an impact on our health. Undoubtedly, these and other reasons impede the ability to express our views and engage in constructive exchanges about our differences. As a consequence, we may give in, avoid conflict, or accommodate the other person's needs without really wanting to do so.

If you have fears about being in conflict, here are some questions to consider regarding a specific dispute (past or present) and how to overcome them. The idea is to reflect on what there is to be learned that will help you cope more effectively during conflict, if your fears tend to dominate your thinking at these times.

QUESTIONS

- How would you describe your fears about the particular dispute you have in mind? What does your answer or answers to this question say about your hopes, expectations, and needs with respect to the situation? What does it (or they) say about your hopes, expectations, and needs regarding your relationship with the other person?

- What two other words describe the impact on you of this particular dispute? How are your fears manifested outwardly? How are you experiencing them inwardly?

- What thoughts were going on for you when the fears first set in?

- Which of the fears that you are experiencing has or have a basis in reality? Which fear or fears may not have a basis in reality?

- In what ways are your fears helping you in this conflict? How are they helping the other person? How are your fears *not* helping you? How are they *not* helping the other person?

- What decision(s) are you making, or have you made, about the conflict that is or are likely fear-based?

- If you want to reduce or eliminate your fears in this situation, what do you think needs to happen to accomplish that? How will you make this happen? What differences would there be if you have no fears in this conflict? If you want to hold onto your fears, why is that so?

- When you consider your answers to the questions here, in what conflict-masterful ways might you proceed regarding this particular dispute?

- Going forward, who would you be without fears in your conflicts? What would you do differently if you were fearless? What other differences would there be if you had no fears?

- What are you learning on this topic that will help you during future conflicts, if you experience fears emerging?

- What else occurs to you as you consider these questions?

- What insights do you have?

Fighting When in Conflict

Many factors determine the approach we take, and the extent to which we react, when we are provoked. Fighting is one way of reacting, and many people equate interpersonal conflict with it. We may have different ideas about what fighting means, as suggested by the other terms commonly associated with it—arguing, yelling, swearing, confronting, challenging. (Remember, as stated in Chapter 1, this book does not include physical conflict, such as hitting, shoving, and so on.)

Fighting in interpersonal conflict is one way to cope, and the motivation to choose this option is often habitual—layered with historical and learned behaviors. A range of other influences inform the choice to fight, too, including the need to feel powerful, to win, and to be and be seen as "stronger." Some other variables that may compel us to fight have to do with who the other person is, how hurt we feel, the stakes of not getting what we want, how important the relationship and issues are to us, and other such concerns.

Things we say when we fight, and how we say them, are often rife with inflammatory words that offend and incite, and that linger after the conflict is over. Yelling, aggressive facial and body language, and other threatening stances may accompany what is being said or shouted. As a result of such ways of interacting, issues get distorted and displaced. Old hurts resurface. Positions become entrenched. Emotional scars are formed or become deeper, and so on. Essentially, what is being fought for and why seem to remain unanswered and unresolved as reason escapes us and we argue from a place of anger and other strong emotions. In the end, fighting consumes much energy and adds increased negativity, tension, and discord to the interpersonal dynamic.

Because we have the ability to change our habitual reactions, it helps to explore a tendency to fight, and to consider alternative ways of being in conflict that more positively influence the route our dispute takes. The following questions will have particular appeal if you are inclined to fight. (The topic **Picking Fights** in Chapter 2 discusses this way of managing conflict before it arises, and has some relevance here.)

Bringing to mind a current or past conflict in which you are fighting or have fought will help you answer the following questions. The present tense is used, though you may find the past tense more applicable.

QUESTIONS

- When you consider a disagreement in which you are fighting with the other person, how would you describe the specific ways you are doing so?

- What, in particular, are you fighting for in this dispute? Why is that so?

- If the other person is fighting back or instigated the fight, what in particular is she or he fighting for? Why is that so?

- If the other person is *not* fighting back, what is she or he doing? What is that like for you that she or he is not fighting back? What is it like for the other person, from what you observe?

- If you win the fight in this situation, what will that mean for you? What will it feel like? What might it mean for the other person?

- If you lose the fight, what will that mean for you? What will it feel like? What will it mean for the other person?

- What, for you, makes fighting the optimal approach regarding this conflict? What do you worry might happen if you do not fight?

- What outcome do you wish for this conflict?

- What other ways of interacting in this conflict may be more suitable, considering what you wish to happen?

- Going forward, instead of fighting, what ways of interacting during conflict are more aligned with how you want to be and be seen?

- What else occurs to you as you consider these questions?

- What insights do you have?

When Silence Is Golden

The exact origin of the expression "silence is golden" is not definite, but the first known use was by the poet Thomas Carlyle, who translated the phrase from German in *Sartor Resartus* in 1831[11]: "speech is silver, silence is golden." In an effort to increase conflict intelligence, it helps to consider how and when this expression applies, and what is needed to use golden moments of silence effectively in our conflicts.

Being present, and attentively hearing what the other person is saying, goes a long way in any circumstance. It is especially critical when we are in the heat of conflict, as it is easy to lose focus and stop listening at these times. Being silent and hearing what the other person says demonstrates that we are curious and open to understanding, rather than being reactive and having to push our own views. The combination of remaining curious and silent opens up the possibility that we learn something important about the other person and the situation that we may not have known previously. Listening, then, benefits both of us.

This is not to say do not talk when in conflict. It does, however, suggest the benefits of waiting and listening to hear where the other person is coming from before responding and providing our perspective. Though we may not always like what we hear, remaining silent as the other person talks through her or his views, assumptions, and reactions helps us to gain clarity. That is, we not only gain increased understanding about her or his perspective. We also become clearer about our own interpretations, attributions, and ideas. Silence is golden at these times.

You may ask, "When is silence *not* golden?" It is not golden when it is used as a way to ignore, avoid, dismiss, or put down the other person. The "silent treatment,"[12] as such an approach is sometimes called, is demonstrated with body language and a demeanor that implicitly state, "You have nothing to say that I want to hear," "I have nothing to say to you," or "you are not worthy of my time, energy, or attention."

When you answer the following questions, it helps to consider a specific conflict in which silence may have been a preferable choice rather than what you said during the interaction.

QUESTIONS

- For what reasons did you *not* remain silent in the dispute you have in mind (if you now recognize that silence would have been preferable)?

- To what, specifically, did you react at the time rather than remain silent?

- Why was what was said or done especially difficult to hear or see? If "difficult" is not the appropriate word, what term is more applicable?

- How did you react in that situation—for example, what did you say or do rather than remain silent? What difference do you think it might have made if you had remained silent and heard out the other person?

- What do you suppose you did *not* hear because you reacted? If this question applies, what do you suppose you did not want to hear?

- When others are silent while you talk, how does that positively affect you? How is it a negative experience for you?

- What are the challenges for you about remaining silent during a conflict and listening to what the other person is saying before you speak?

- Generally, how would you complete this sentence within the conflict context: "When I am silent, I fear…"? In what way(s) is that fear (or those fears) relevant to the conflict you discussed here? How realistic is that fear (those fears)?

- Generally, how would you complete this sentence within the conflict context: "When I am silent, I feel as though…"? What does that feeling mean for you in this conflict?

- What do you think talking achieves that silence does not? What do you think silence achieves that talking does not? What are you learning here about the use of silence in conflict that is new to you?

- What else occurs to you as you consider these questions?

- What insights do you have?

The Straw That Broke the Camel's Back

The expression "the straw that broke the camel's back" generally describes something that pushes an ongoing situation too far. According to Wikipedia, this idiom is from an Arabic proverb about "how a camel is loaded beyond its capacity to move or stand." It is a "reference to any process by which cataclysmic failure (a broken back) is achieved by a seemingly inconsequential addition, a single straw." This expression also gives rise to the phrase "the last or final straw," used "when something is deemed to be the last in a line of unacceptable occurrences."[13]

The metaphor—"the straw that breaks the camel's back"—as it applies to conflict may arise when an offence is so noxious that it triggers an excessive reaction, or when a repeated behavior reaches a point at which it is too much to tolerate. Or, we have simply had enough discord and are fed up with the situation and the other person such that the slightest gesture or statement crosses the line of acceptance. (A related topic, **Boundary Considerations in a Conflict Conversation** in Chapter 2, also refers to this phenomenon.)

These and other dynamics of conflict—when things have gone too far for one or the other of us—often lead to reactions that escalate or prolong the conflict. For instance, we may overreact by yelling, cursing, criticizing, name-calling, and blurting out things we regret. Or, we may shut down altogether.

If this has happened to you or is happening in a current situation—where it could be said a straw broke, or is breaking, the camel's back—the following questions will help to deconstruct what occurred.

QUESTIONS

- What, specifically, did the other person say or do that represents the "straw" for you in that situation? What does the "camel's back" represent about you?

- What happened as a consequence of the other person's provoking you to the extent she or he did?

- What sorts of things had built up between you two prior to this that might have contributed to that outcome (your answer to the previous question)?

- At what point could the other person have done or said something differently that would not have resulted in the negative turn that occurred? What might she or he have done or said? How might that have prevented things from going too far?

- What may have precluded her or him from doing or saying what you suggested (in the second part of the previous question) at that time?

- What was the "straw" for the other person that broke her or his back in that situation—if that happened? What does the "camel's back" represent about her or him?

- At what point might you have said or done something differently? What might you have said or done?

- How might that have worked (your answer to the previous question)? What stopped you from saying or doing that at the time?

- What do you intend to do in the future to prevent a straw from breaking the camel's back for the other person?

- What do you intend to do in the future to prevent a straw from breaking your own back? How do you intend to respond in conflict-masterful ways if the other person does wield a straw of some sort that has the potential for breaking your back?

- What else occurs to you as you consider these questions?

- What insights do you have?

Reconnecting During a Dispute

We often say that a relationship "breaks down" during a dispute. When you think about it, we do disconnect from one another in many ways at these times. We also lose connection with our own feelings and thoughts. When this happens, it is difficult to imagine that things can be mended.

Losing connection with others, especially people we care about, is an uncomfortable, unnerving, and stressful place to be. Some of us experience mournful feelings, grieving that the relationship may be irreparable. We may experience anxiety and a sense of helplessness at these times. These sorts of emotions and thoughts are often the reason some people avoid conflict (also see **Fears About Being in Conflict**, earlier in this chapter).

Figuring out how to reconnect with the other person—in the midst of an interpersonal dispute when we sense that things are breaking down—can be challenging. In the quest for conflict mastery, it helps to consider when a schism is beginning to form in order to prevent it from widening. Remaining mindful about when the signs appear, and how they present themselves, will be our ongoing reminder to step back, focus on our intentions, and tap into our instincts. (**Acting on Simmering Signs** or **Picking Up the Conflict Vibes** are two related topics in Chapter 2, and **Mending Fences** in Chapter 4 also discusses reconnecting after conflict.)

Furthermore, staying connected or reconnecting with ourselves is every bit as crucial, and integral to staying grounded and centered during a conflict. It is also pivotal to preventing a breakdown of the relationship. Among other things, reconnecting with ourselves and the other person at these times also means identifying what is important to us, individually and collectively.

The following questions aim to facilitate the possibility of reconnecting with yourself and the other person during a conflict as soon as you sense things are beginning to break down.

QUESTIONS

- When you consider a dispute in which you have begun to experience a disconnect from the other person, what do you think started the schism? How are you experiencing the initial signs of disconnecting?

- How may you describe the disconnect within yourself? What does that feel like, if you have not stated this yet?

- What do you observe or sense that the disconnection between you and the other person is like for her or him?

- How do you want to feel about the other person when you reconnect? How do you want her or him to feel about you? How do you want to feel about yourself?

- What do you want to know or understand about the other person and what is going on for her or him to be able to reconnect?

- What do you need from the other person to be able to reconnect with her or him? How will you express that and any other needs in a conflict-masterful way that demonstrates your desire to reconnect?

- What might the other person *not* know and understand about you that will facilitate her or his reconnection with you?

- What do you think will help you reconnect with yourself that you have not mentioned yet? What else do you think will help you reconnect with the other person?

- What image or metaphor best describes what the reconnection with the other person will feel, look, or be like when you make it?

- How might you salvage connections in the future when you begin to disconnect from yourself because of an interpersonal conflict? What conflict-masterful approach will you use to salvage the connection when you begin to sense a disconnect with the other person?

- What else occurs to you as you consider these questions?

- What insights do you have?

CHAPTER FOUR

After Conflict

After Conflict—Some Preliminary Thoughts to Consider

Various aspects of what occurs during some of our interpersonal conflicts may remain for long periods of time in our head, heart, and body. Sometimes our lingering thoughts and emotions get in the way of moving forward, and we feel stuck about how to relate to the other person. We may try to pretend things are all right but know, at some level of awareness, that is not the case. The lack of authenticity we are feeling about how we are communicating and interacting, when this happens, is uncomfortable and anxiety-provoking.

The sorts of things that seep into our consciousness after our conflicts are over—and that prolong our recovery—may be unspoken words and unreconciled issues and conversations. We may replay, over and over, all or parts of the interaction that upset us. We may become confused and unclear about who said or did what. In the sharing with others we may convey what we wished we had said or done and play down what we did say or do. We even come to believe the different versions of the situation that come out of our mouth.

What often has a continuing and strong impact on us and our relationships after conflict are emotions associated with the things that stay with us. Our regrets, guilt, shame, hurt, resentment, anger, sadness, despair, embarrassment, or other feelings about the other person, ourselves, and what transpired prey on us. Our connection with the other person may feel broken, engendering feelings of loss. We long to be more at peace within ourselves but feel unsettled and unresolved.

Other lingering vestiges that may also have an impact on our health, happiness, and general well-being take the form of blaming ourselves for what we did not say or could have said differently. Or, we may remain in blame about the other person's contribution to the discord and attribute actions and words that are not hers or his to own. We may carry a grudge. We may worry about our lack of resilience—that we are not bouncing back—realizing that, too, is having a negative impact on us and those around us. It is even the case that we overreact when the same type of dynamic that provokes us in one conflict occurs with someone else. Or, as a consequence of continuing angst, we may be generally more sensitive, defensive, and reactive.

Considering all this, it is evident that after-conflict ruminations typically arise because of things that we did not manage as well as we would have preferred during conflict. They may even reverberate back to the time before conflict, when our choices about how to be and interact first present themselves. What this chapter will illuminate, then, is the learning to be gained by examining our disputes in retrospect. That is, until and even after we gain conflict mastery, there are benefits in analyzing any lasting aftereffects. For instance, we have an opportunity at these times to contemplate what we have learned and consider ways to manage aspects of our conflicts that remain undone or were not done well.

With this in mind, the topics and questions in this chapter are designed to shed light on the range of dynamics that frequently occur after interpersonal conflicts. This often entails reflecting back on what happened before or during their evolution. Accordingly, some questions ask you to deconstruct what occurred to be able to reconstruct what needs to happen to engage in conflict with increased mastery. They also aim to facilitate the ability to take off the remnants that continue to cling to you so they do not impede forward movement. Essentially, the questions and topics are meant to provide insights on what there is to learn from things we hang onto about our conflicts to help us manage future ones more effectively.

This final chapter will be of special interest to those who feel unresolved after a dispute—cognitively, physically, emotionally, spiritually, and otherwise. It will resonate if you have trouble reconciling the things that arise in interpersonal conflicts that do not dissipate after they are over. The topics and questions will also have meaning for people who strive to get over and beyond what happens in conflicts that may impede our moving ahead. Similarly, they will help you to acknowledge your sensibilities about being in conflict, and to recognize what you already do that works, what does not work, and on what to focus your energies in the quest for conflict intelligence and mastery.

Post-Conflict Agony

In the aftermath of interpersonal conflicts, those of us who tend to agonize about what happened do so in various ways. We may make the situation bigger than it was owing to ongoing emotions that prevail. Or, we may try to minimize it while suppressing or trying to suppress the impact. We may ruminate about unresolved hurts and issues—dwelling on our feelings to the point of becoming depleted and depressed. At times our agonizing may even demonstrate a need to hold onto the pain and not forgive the other person or ourselves. These and other examples of post-conflict reactions have many layers to them.

Post-conflict agony, in whatever form it takes and for whatever reasons it aches, is especially debilitating when it keeps us in a negative place and from moving on. What is more, post-conflict agony often contributes to carrying grudges (to be discussed later in this chapter), ongoing tension, physical and emotional signs of stress, and repeating behaviors that we do not like about ourselves and which do not serve us well.

The questions that follow will help you consider and unpack some of the layers in one of your specific conflicts and generally, if you are inclined to agonize in the aftermath of conflict. They are also designed to help you gain more awareness about how this tendency affects you and the interrelational dynamic.

QUESTIONS

- If you are agonizing about a previous conflict, what sorts of thoughts continue to stay with you? For what reasons are you agonizing about these particular things?

- What specific words describe the emotions you are experiencing? How are you otherwise affected? In what ways do you think you are showing your emotions?

- How are your post-conflict emotions affecting the other person, as far as you can tell? How are they affecting the relationship?

- What did you need from the other person during the conflict that, if you had it (then), might have reduced or eliminated the agony you are now experiencing? What do you need from her or him now?

- What do you think you might have said or done differently during the conflict to have lessened your post-conflict agony?

- If you gain something from agonizing after this conflict, what are you gaining? If you are losing something, what are you losing?

- There might be commonalities and patterns regarding the things you are agonizing about in the aftermath of this interpersonal conflict as compared to others about which you have also agonized, or are still agonizing. If so, what commonalities and patterns are you aware of?

- When you observe others—for example, friends or family—agonizing after conflict, what sorts of observations have you made of them? What input do you offer to them at these times? Or, if you do not do so but think about advice or other things you would like to suggest, what would that be? How does the input you just referred to resonate as something else you might want or need yourself to help move past the agony you are experiencing?

- Now that you have thought about it, what will help you move past the agony that you have not considered yet? What will the indicators be that you are ready to let go of the agony?

- What do you intend to do differently during future interpersonal conflicts that will preclude agonizing afterwards?

- What else occurs to you as you consider these questions?

- What insights do you have?

Understanding Why We Blame

During interpersonal conflicts, we human beings have the capacity to say and do awful things to defend ourselves and hurt the other person. Some conduct is inexcusable. When we are on the receiving end of mean, thoughtless, rude, and other such behaviors, we cope in different ways in the aftermath. Depending on many variables, including how egregious we consider the words and actions to be, some of us are able to move on quicker than others. Some of us choose to hold on indefinitely. And some of us take a long time to get over and past the experience. When it takes a protracted period of time, we often spend much energy blaming the other person.

Along with finding fault, some of us may be inclined to retaliate. Others may make excuses for our part and demonize the other person in different ways to justify our actions. We may exaggerate the truth of what the other person said or did. Our perceptions—blown out of proportion at these times—become our new reality, and before we know it, the situation becomes increasingly distorted in our memory and the telling.

Because we know intellectually that blaming does not make things better, it helps in the quest for conflict mastery to gain clarity about what compels an inclination to blame and even stay in that place for a long time. We may start by asking ourselves "yes–no" questions such as, "Am I angry that the conflict remains unresolved?," "Did I hope she would say or do something more conciliatory?," "Do I want to hurt the other person back?," or "Do I want him to admit something or take the responsibility for what happened?"

Asking ourselves these sorts of questions is helpful when figuring out why we continue to blame the other person after the conflict is over and what unmet expectations we are aware of. Here are some reflective questions that will help shed more light on a tendency to find fault, if you are inclined to do so or are blaming someone in a specific dispute.

QUESTIONS

- For what, specifically, are you blaming the other person regarding the dispute you have in mind? Why are you doing so?

- What sorts of questions (such as those referred to in the third paragraph on this topic) are you asking yourself about your expectations of the other person? What do your questions mean regarding the reason(s) you continue to blame her or him?

- If the other person is not aware of what you are blaming her or him for, why is that so? Whether or not the other person knows, what impact is the fact that you continue to blame her or him having on the relationship? What impact does blaming the other person have on you?

- What do you believe about the other person (her or his character, history, personality, and so on) that supports your blameful reaction in this situation? On what are you basing that belief or those beliefs about her or him?

- What do you wish the other person had said or done differently at the time of the conflict that might have contributed to a more positive outcome? Why do you suppose she or he did not do so?

- If the other person is outwardly blaming you for something, what is that? For what might the other person be blaming you that she or he is not telling you? What might she or he wish you had done differently that might have contributed to a more positive outcome? What do you wish you had said or done?

- What difference does it make whether or not you blame the other person?

- What would it take for you to let go of the blame you are feeling about the other person in this conflict? If you prefer to hold onto the blame—at least for now— why is that so?

- In the past, what conflict-masterful approaches have worked to help you move past blame? What effective approaches have you used before or during previous conflicts such that you have *not* ended up blaming the other person? How may these approaches apply (or have applied) in this case?

- When will you know you are ready to let go of the blame? How will things be different in your relationship with the other person when you stop blaming her or him? What do you expect it will feel like when you stop blaming her or him?

- What else occurs to you as you consider these questions?

- What insights do you have?

Observing Ourselves Through Someone Else's Eyes

It is strange to think about what we look like when we are in conflict. However, considering how we physically show up in our conflicts helps us become more conscious of how our appearance and way of being contribute to the discord. Similarly, paying attention to how the other person appears during our conflicts further increases our awareness about the impact of non-verbal forms of expression on the interaction. (If this topic is of interest to you, you may want to consider other related topics. Chapter 2 addresses various somatic signs evident in some conflicts, such as **The Cold Shoulder**, **Chip on the Shoulder**, and **That Put My Back Up**. Chapter 3 discusses the **Body and Facial Language of Conflict**.)

In the aftermath of conflict, it is feasible—at least to some extent—to reflect back and describe our demeanor, including the look on our face, our body language, and how we acted. And taking some time to examine when certain counterproductive mannerisms appear helps us to focus on what specifically evokes them. Doing so also gives us a chance to explore our triggers and consider what it would take to become more masterful in expressing our reactions when they are activated.

One way of exploring how we appear when we are in conflict and how it adds to the dissension is to imagine someone special to us is watching as we interact. With that in mind, the line of inquiry here works well if you begin by recalling a conflict between you and another person in which you are aware, or have been told, that your body and face reflected unproductive signs of engagement. Once you have that recollection, envision that you were observed by two or more close and caring friends, family members, or colleagues, as you respond to the following questions.

QUESTIONS

- To the extent you are able to do so, how would you describe your overall physical appearance that reflected negative reactions in the conflict you brought to mind? More specifically, how might you describe your body language? What expression was on your face? How were you acting?

- To what, specifically, were you reacting when your face, body, or actions were as you described in response to the previous question? At what point did you become aware that your demeanor was demonstrating your discontent, upset, and so on? What words would you use to describe the emotions you were showing other than discontent or upset?

- What do you think was most off-putting for the other person about how you appeared? What might have been most off-putting about how you acted?

- It happens in some interpersonal conflicts that one person mirrors the other person's body and facial language and way of interacting. If you mirrored the other person in any of these ways, how did you do so? How might she or he have mirrored your facial and body language and way of interacting? What is there to be learned from this sort of dynamic?

- How might caring observers (friends, family, and so on) describe your body and facial language in that conflict? How might they say you acted that would be the same as you described? How might they describe how you acted in different ways (pertaining to your response to the first question in this series)? What words might they use to describe the emotions they observed or heard from you?

- How did you appear or act in that incident that you would be embarrassed about in front of your caring observers? What might surprise them most about your facial or body language? What might surprise them about how you acted? What would the observers support and applaud about how you were in that conflict?

- What pieces of advice might your observers suggest as more conflict-masterful ways you could have interacted?

- What observations have you made of others in conflict that you would *not* want to emulate—such as their body and facial language? About the way they act?

- What have you seen in others whom you have observed in conflict that you admire?

- In future, what do you intend to do differently about how you look and act in interpersonal conflicts to be perceived as more masterful?

- What else occurs to you as you consider these questions?

- What insights do you have?

Carrying Grudges

Grudges refer to a tendency to hold onto negative feelings about the other person and things we attribute to her or him, and some of us carry them at length after certain conflicts. Though we are aware that doing so precludes full reconciliation—and does not otherwise serve us well—we may have trouble shedding the inclination, and getting over what upset us.

What reasons may there be for carrying grudges? We may carry grudges because the issues remain unresolved, and we had hoped for a more satisfying outcome. We may carry grudges due to a general lack of resilience, or a tendency to blame or self-criticize and see ourselves as a victim. We may be unable to effectively process parts or all of what happened in the conflict, owing to the ongoing emotions we are experiencing. It may be because we cannot stop thinking about what the other person said or did that offended us. Or, maybe she or he moved on in a way that we perceive as lack of caring or remorse.

These and other reasons contribute to ongoing discord and tension, internally and externally. In either case, we might demonstrate we are carrying grudges by ignoring the person, or making derogatory and fault-finding remarks about her or him. We may seek revenge. We may remain unsettled—on edge, sullen, nervous, and anxious around the other person. We may appear guarded and untrusting. We may withdraw into ourselves. **Post-Conflict Agony** and **Understanding Why We Blame** in this chapter also speak to this topic to some extent.

At times, underneath our grudges there may be caring feelings that we are not always conscious of. For instance, we may care about the issues in dispute—imagining an outcome that reconciled our differences more satisfactorily. We may care about the relationship and hope we can mend the rift. We may be wishing that things will return to the way they were before, and we are missing the connection we used to have with the other person. Identifying whatever it is we are or were caring about in our conflicts, then, is as useful to consider—if not more so—as the grudge we are carrying.

Based on these thoughts, the following questions aim to increase insights about holding grudges and the caring that may underlie these feelings with regard to a past conflict.

QUESTIONS

- In general, under what circumstances do you tend to carry grudges (if you do)?

- When you consider one conflict situation in which you are carrying a grudge, how would you describe what the grudge is about? What does it feel like to carry this grudge?

- What are you caring about with respect to the situation and issues in dispute? What are the specific emotions fueling the grudge?

- What are you caring about with respect to the other person? How did the other person's actions or words during the conflict challenge that feeling? What is she or he doing now that you perceive as an ongoing challenge to your relationship?

- What do you want the other person to care about that you do not think she or he does?

- How does the other person experience your grudge, from what you can tell? What do you think she or he does *not* realize that you are caring about regarding your relationship? What might she or he not realize you are caring about with respect to the issues between you?

- What are you realizing you care about that you were not aware of when you began to answer this set of questions?

- Perhaps you prefer to hold onto the grudge. If so, why is that? What does that grudge suggest you care about? What does it mean going forward?

- When you have let go of grudges you were carrying in other situations, what helped you to do so? If you want to let go of the grudge in this situation, what do you think it will take for you to do so?

- What signs will indicate you are ready to let go of this grudge? What will be different when you let go? What will you care about once you have let go of this grudge?

- What else occurs to you as you consider these questions?

- What insights do you have?

The Weight of Conflict

We carry the weight of our conflicts in many different ways. The fact itself of having had an altercation can weigh us down. And with some situations, we limp along indefinitely with the emotional repercussions firmly packed in our heart and mind along with bad memories, unfulfilled expectations, and unresolved issues. Together, these things can feel like a heavy load to carry.

When the ongoing weight of conflict stays with us, we may ask ourselves questions that may be self-limiting or blameful, such as: "Why did I let myself get into that?"; "What was I trying to prove?"; "Why did I react so strongly to what was she saying?"; "Why did he get so upset?"; "What got into her that she became so irate?"; or "Who does he think he is anyway—blaming me for what he did?" Such questions add to the continuing burden we experience about what occurred in our conflicts, and they have an oppressive impact on us and the relationship.

As a consequence of becoming preoccupied with the conflict and worrying about the continuing weight we carry, we may also sense its heaviness push against us in other unsettling ways. That is, the weight may show up in aches and pains, in fatigue, in feelings of sadness, loss, and despair, in sleeplessness, and in relentless thoughts about what we should have said or done. These and numerous other sensations add to the weight that keeps us from moving forward. (See the previous topic, **Carrying Grudges**.)

The following reflective questions are ones to consider when past conflicts are over, for all intents and purposes, but seem still to weigh you down. They are designed to help identify and unload at least some of the weight of a conflict that continues to feel heavy.

QUESTIONS

- What particularly is weighing you down about the conflict you brought to mind? What would you say the reasons are? Besides the word "heavy," what other words describe the weight?

- What sorts of questions are you asking yourself about this conflict (such as in paragraph two above)? What do your answers to the questions say about what you are feeling with regard to the other person? About the conflict? About yourself?

- How many idiomatic kilograms or pounds would you attribute to the weight you are carrying regarding this conflict? What do the kilograms or pounds consist of? What would be a more tolerable weight? What would that weight be made of?

- In what ways is it evident to you that you are carrying the weight? How might bystanders describe how you are being or appear because of the weight you are carrying?

- If you are able to compartmentalize the weight, what part feels heaviest? What do you believe makes that the heaviest?

- What do you want ultimately to feel about the conflict so that it will no longer weigh you down? What do you want to feel about yourself?

- What do you want to feel about the other person instead of what you feel now, due to the weight of the conflict? What do you want her or him to feel about you?

- If there is something comforting, or comfortable, or otherwise positive you are experiencing from carrying the weight, what is that?

- What is one thing you might unpack from the weight today to start to lighten the load, if you are ready to do so? Going forward, what else do you intend to do to lighten the weight you are carrying?

- If answering this set of questions has reduced the weight of the conflict at all, how has it done so? How much weight are you now carrying (compared to your answer to the third question on this topic)? What did you specifically unpack to lighten the load? What will you do next to further reduce the weight of this conflict?

- What else occurs to you as you consider these questions?

- What insights do you have?

Regrets After Conflict

Even when an interpersonal dispute appears to be resolved, there are times when some of us continue to feel that matters are not fully reconciled. There are many reasons this occurs, and sometimes they have to do with the regrets we carry. We may regret saying or doing some things that we know were inappropriate, hurtful, thoughtless, and so on. Or, we repeat in our heads the unspoken words and sentiments we wish we had expressed. Or, we blame ourselves that we did not accommodate the other person's needs more than our own to avoid further dissension.

Having these and other regrets about what happened in a conflict is a lousy feeling. Regrets are challenging to shed and add further layers to the initial conflict. Ruminations of this nature generally trigger a range of unsettling reactions that grow inside us such as self-blame, guilt, embarrassment, and shame. At times, we may imagine or fabricate things about the conflict and the other person in an effort to reduce our regrets. This may include passing on the blame to her or him, rationalizing and making excuses for ourselves, trying to elicit support from friends, including mutual ones, by bad-mouthing the other person, and using other methods we hope will make us feel less remorse.

There are many other consequences that accompany remorseful feelings. They deplete our energy and cause ongoing distress for us and tension with the other person. Those around us may also experience the reverberations. The previous discussions on **Post-Conflict Agony**, **Understanding Why We Blame**, **The Weight of Conflict**, and the next topic on **Post-Conflict Guilt** also speak to the impact of regrets when a conflict is ostensibly over.

The fact is, we sometimes say and do things during conflict that do not reflect who and how we want to be in the situation or the relationship. It may seem as though we step out of ourselves and react in ways that are uncharacteristic. They surprise and disappoint us and the other person.

In the end, regretting what we said or did—or did not say or do—does not serve us well. Yet, acknowledging the remorse and considering what it is about provide an opportunity to learn and apply the knowledge gained from this conflict so that we do not repeat regret-causing actions in the future. The following questions aim to facilitate that learning.

QUESTIONS

- What did you say or do—or not say or do—in a specific conflict situation about which you now have regrets?

- What bothers you most about having those regrets? In what other ways are you bothered? If the words "bothers" and "bothered" do not resonate, what words might you use instead to describe the emotional impact?

- If you were to have the chance to redo the situation, what would you say or do that you would *not* regret? If something stopped you from saying or doing that at the time, why do you suppose that was?

- How might the outcome have been different if you had said or done those things you referred to in the last question? What else would be different?

- What did you need from the other person that you did not have before or during the conflict? What did you need from yourself?

- What similarities, if any, are there about your regrets in this situation compared to other incidents when you experienced regret? What is different? How do you interpret the similarities? How do you interpret the differences?

- Which regrets about this situation provide important lessons for you to carry forward? What are the exact lessons? What positive things did you learn about yourself in this situation?

- What skills and ways of being in conflict have you observed in others that you would like to incorporate into your quest for conflict mastery in order to reduce the possibility of regrets in future conflicts? What have you learned from your own past experiences that will be of assistance?

- How do you want to feel after a conflict, instead of having regrets?

- Going forward, what other conflict-masterful options—besides those you have already described—do you intend to use that will result in having those feelings (your answer to the previous question)?

- What else occurs to you as you consider these questions?

- What insights do you have?

Post-Conflict Guilt

According to Wikipedia, the term "guilt" means "a cognitive or an emotional experience that occurs when a person realizes or believes—accurately or not—that he or she has compromised his or her own standards of conduct or has violated a moral standard, and bears significant responsibility for that violation."[1]

Feelings of guilt may emerge after conflict for a range of reasons—for example, we may believe we contributed to the discord by offending or hurting the other person. We may have been obnoxious, rude, demeaning, insulting, or degrading. We may have withheld a truth. We may have retaliated, gossiped, or acted in our self-interest. Such actions may haunt us after the conflict and lead to remorse and continuing self-blame. **Post-Conflict Agony**, **Regrets After Conflict**, and **Considering the Consequences of What We Say** touch on this topic, too.

When we feel guilty after a conflict, we may repeatedly play the scenario over in our head and continually berate ourselves. We may blame the other person and focus anger at her or him. We may attempt to compensate for what we said or did by placating her or him—being overly solicitous and making efforts to get back into the other person's good graces. We may rationalize and over-explain what we said or did and why, or make excuses to justify our actions. We may act as though matters are resolved and have reverted back to how they were before the conflict—even when that clearly is not the case.

If you feel guilty about a specific situation, the following questions will provide ways to examine your ongoing feelings in this regard. The questions also invite you to consider ways to avoid guilt in future conflicts.

Courtesy of CINERGY Coaching (www.cinergycoaching.com). This page may be reproduced to enhance your use of this workbook.

QUESTIONS

- What do you feel guilty about with respect to the situation you have in mind? What two words describe your emotions about this situation other than "guilt"?

- In what specific ways does the concept of guilt—as defined in the first paragraph of this topic—apply to the guilt you are experiencing in this conflict? What in this definition does *not* apply to you?

- What might you add to the definition to define guilt as you are experiencing it?

- When you consider the consequences that can arise when guilt prevails after a conflict (such as those suggested in the third paragraph of this topic), which might apply to you? What might you add to this list?

- What admission have you not voiced that may be contributing to your feelings of guilt (if this is applicable)? How might sharing it with the other person alleviate your guilt? How might making that admission *not* help matters?

- What is effective about how you are managing your guilt? What is not effective?

- What conflict-masterful ways can you think of to manage the guilt?

- When you get over your guilt, what will you have gotten over? What will be on the other side of your guilt?

- When you think about it now, what lessons might be learned from post-conflict guilt?

- What might you do about how you interact in future conflicts that would not induce guilt in you?

- What else occurs to you as you consider these questions?

- What insights do you have?

Second-Guessing the Conflict

Sometimes after a dispute is over we second-guess what we said or did. Sentences that express this tendency often start with, "If I had only…," "I wish I had…," and "Why didn't I…?" The very expression "second-guessing" suggests that we made a first guess about what to say or do, and we are now doubting its wisdom.

When we look back after a conflict—with the benefit of hindsight—we often have an understanding we did not have at the time and wish we'd had. Sometimes we've obtained information we did not have before. Or, we realize we missed an opportunity to get it. We may have acted on assumptions, or without thinking about the consequences. Or, we are feeling more clear-headed now and better able to explore the underpinnings of the dispute and our contribution to its evolution.

How *not* to second-guess ourselves in our conflicts requires some forethought. This means, for instance, reflecting on what we want as an outcome, and setting our intentions before raising or responding to a potentially contentious matter. The topics **Preparing to Initiate a Conflict Conversation** and **Preparing to Respond in a Conflict Conversation** in Chapter 2 discuss intentions in this context, too. To some extent, the previous two topics—**Regrets After Conflict** and **Post-Conflict Guilt**—also address the concept of second-guessing and will be helpful in examining this propensity.

If, after conflict, you are inclined to second-guess what you said or did, the following questions will help to deconstruct this tendency.

QUESTIONS

- What are you second-guessing that you said or did in the dispute you have in mind? What are your reasons for second-guessing?

- What is it like to second-guess? What specific emotions have you experienced about second-guessing in the dispute you are considering?

- What motivated your "first guess" in that situation—what you said or did in the first place—that you are now doubting? What else might have influenced you at the time?

- What were you feeling about the other person at the time? What do you feel about her or him now?

- What were you feeling about yourself at the time of the conflict? What do you feel about yourself now?

- What do you know now that you did not know at the time of the conflict that is relevant to the issues? Relevant to the other person? How might you have known these things at the time?

- When you hear others second-guessing, what do you think? What might you want to say to them that is a good lesson to consider now about your own second-guessing?

- What have you learned from this particular dispute about what you are (or were) second-guessing?

- What else might there be to learn about second-guessing that will help in your efforts to gain conflict mastery?

- Going forward, how might you make a first choice in an interaction—about what to say and do or how—that would *not* result in second-guessing?

- What else occurs to you as you consider these questions?

- What insights do you have?

Conflict Conversation Readiness

Often, we make an effort to communicate with the other person after a conflict but before we are ready—or before she or he is ready. Anxiety to resolve the issues, a desire to get past the high emotions or ongoing dissension, a need to reconcile and make amends, and other reasons compel many of us to dive in prematurely. On the other hand, we may wait too long before we reach out.

Deciding when to initiate a potentially challenging conversation, and being unsure about the best approach, may contribute to prolonging matters. At these times—when we delay for a protracted period—we may then find our efforts are perceived as "too little, too late" despite our good intentions.

Poor timing—whether too early or too late—can have an impact on how amenable the other person (or we) will be to talk through a conflict and see whether reconciliation is even feasible. Contemplating how and when to discuss an incident takes some thought. It also takes checking in with ourselves and the other person to consider our own and their readiness before proceeding.

Checking out our own readiness involves many variables such as the emotions we continue to feel, and whether we have begun to forgive ourselves and the other person for things said or done. It means reflecting on our part of the interaction, too. It is also a matter of clarifying what we hope to achieve in a conversation with the other person, and what aspects of it require our concentrated preparation.

Checking out the other person's readiness, as in Chapter 2: **Preparing to Respond in a Conflict Conversation**, may take different forms, depending on our style. Some approaches—made soon after the conflict—might sound like: "I'd really like to talk this through with you and I hope you do, too. Right now, I'd appreciate time to think it out first. When is a good time for you?" Or, "Will you please let me know when you would like to discuss what happened?" Or, "I would like a day or two before discussing what happened. How about you?"

For this series of questions, it will help to think about a situation in which you approached the other person and realized that it was too soon after the dispute, and another when someone approached you and it was too early from your perspective. You might also consider a situation in which the approach was made too late, either for the other person or for you.

QUESTIONS

- When you approached the other person to discuss your conflict, and realized she or he was not ready, what was the reaction? How had you determined the timing? From what you could tell, why was it too early? What happened?

- When another person has approached you to discuss a conflict before you were ready, what did you experience? Why were you not yet ready? What happened?

- Generally, what do you consider are the risks of reaching out too early?

- When you approached the other person in another situation and realized the approach came too late for her or him, how had you determined the timing in that case? What made it too late, from what you heard or could tell? What happened?

- If someone has approached you too late after a conflict, how was that for you? What made it too late? What happened?

- In general, what do you consider are the risks of reaching out too late?

- When you reflect on your answers here and your experience, what best practices will guide you going forward, to determine the other person's readiness to discuss a potentially contentious matter?

- What conflict-masterful approach will you use if it is too early and the other person is not ready? If she or he experiences your approach as too late, what conflict-masterful approach will you use in response?

- What usually determines your own readiness to engage in a discussion when the other person approaches you?

- What conflict-masterful response do you intend to use, going forward, at the times you are not ready to discuss matters when the other person approaches you? If you consider the approach too late?

- What else occurs to you as you consider these questions?

- What insights do you have?

Considering the Consequences of What We Say

Some of the negative consequences of disputes have to do with what we say and do. Others are about what we do not say or do. And some unsatisfactory results have to do with our tone of voice, how we act, our attitude, our demeanor, and other communication conveyed non-verbally. Whatever the case, if we have not yet gained conflict mastery, we will not be fully cognizant of what we are expressing and how we are doing so. This likely means, too, we are not aware of how these things are affecting the other person and our interaction.

If we do not respond to the other person, we may be seen as ignoring, dismissing, or avoiding her or him. Such non-verbal messages can be as damaging as those outwardly expressed when we react with words that are mean, thoughtless, and hurtful. Or, we may react in other offensive ways and have to face the fact—too late—that we cannot take back or undo what we said or did. The impact of such interactions can stay with both of us for a long time.

Most of us would agree that thinking before speaking is sage advice. But the phrase is likely spoken more often than practiced. When emotions escalate we lose our equilibrium, and catching ourselves before we speak destructive words is a challenge. However, it is a sign of conflict mastery to be able to regulate our emotions and filter our words by considering our intentions and choices, and anticipating the consequences if we do not. (Regulating emotions was also discussed in Chapter 3: **Understanding Heightened Emotions When in Conflict**.)

Looking back after conflict is a good time to consider what lessons are to be gained from situations when we tend to lose track of ourselves. The following questions are designed to facilitate such a process, with a view to ultimately preventing unproductive outcomes in future conflicts. For this series, it is suggested that you consider a past dispute that has had continuing negative consequences because of words hastily spoken.

QUESTIONS

- In retrospect, what did you say in the dispute you are considering that you would like to take back? What might the other person add or express differently if she or he overheard your answer here?

- What were you intending by what you said (your answers to the above questions)? How might the other person have interpreted your intentions?

- What negative consequences has the other person experienced because of what you said? What are the ongoing negative consequences that you are experiencing because of what you said? What are you feeling about these consequences (your answers to these two questions)?

- What choices did you have about what you could have said that would have had a more positive outcome? What do you think stopped you from saying those things at the time?

- What else might the other person identify as things you could have said that would have had a more positive outcome from her or his perspective?

- What did you hope would happen in this conflict that did not?

- What potential is there for positive consequences to come from this conflict, despite what has occurred so far? What might you say to make that happen?

- What communication skills and inner resources do you already have to help you refrain from speaking potentially damaging words in future conflicts? How will you employ those next time?

- What have you learned about the consequences of your words in this conflict that you will apply to future disputes? What else did you learn?

- How, specifically, will you apply your learning in conflict-masterful ways?

- What else occurs to you as you consider these questions?

- What insights do you have?

Gaining Distance from Hurts

Emotions experienced due to our conflicts can hurt in ways that are often indescribable. Sometimes we hurt so deeply that we experience pain throughout our being—causing us to feel debilitated, physically sick, depressed, empty, sad, and despairing. This type of pain sometimes feels as though it will never go away. Even after our emotions about the conflict, the other person, and ourselves seem to dissipate, they may at times emerge out of nowhere as though the precipitating incident just happened.

Continuing hurts of this nature, after a conflict, are often signs of unreconciled feelings and issues. They may reflect, too, how important the matter was for us and how much we care about the relationship that does not seem quite mended. (Some related aspects are addressed in other topics in this chapter—**Post-Conflict Agony**, **Carrying Grudges**, and **The Weight of Conflict**.)

In circumstances when we stay hurt for long periods of time, it helps to consider ways to gain distance from the conflict dynamic to explore what is going on for us, and what we are holding on to. Without some inner exploration of what we are experiencing and why, the ongoing pain interferes not only with our health and well-being. Our relationship with ourselves, the other person, and sometimes others also suffers, and we have trouble moving on.

The following questions aim to help you gain some distance from ongoing hurts to be able to explore more objectively what is happening for you. You may even discover what is possibly keeping you attached to your hurts and the conflict.

QUESTIONS

- What three other words besides "hurt" describe the emotions that are staying with you about an interpersonal conflict? How are the feelings you just referred to affecting your life? How are your ongoing feelings affecting the other person, as far as you can tell? How are these feelings affecting others, if you know or can tell?

- What would you like to get over or have resolved about the dispute so that you no longer stay hurt, and are able to move on? What is the hardest part of doing so?

- What occurs to you that you could have said or done during the conflict that might have prevented some of the hurt you experienced? How does your answer here affect the challenge of gaining distance from the situation?

- If you do not think you are yet ready to get over the conflict, what is precluding your readiness? What might you be attached to about the interaction? How will you know when you are ready to stop keeping the interaction alive in your mind and heart?

- What idiomatic distance (in kilometers or miles) would you like to have between yourself and the situation that will indicate you are gaining distance and feeling less hurt? What distance from the situation do you feel right now?

- What would be different in your life if you stopped feeling the three emotions you referred to in response to the first question in this set? What three different emotions do you expect to experience once you gain distance from the hurt?

- When you imagine the difference(s) in your life and emotions that you just described in answer to the previous question, what will be especially good? If there is something you do not like about what will be different in your life and emotions, what is that? Why is that so?

- When you are able to stand back from the hurt you are experiencing and begin to gain distance from this conflict, what do you hope the learning will be from this situation that you will carry forward?

- If, by considering the questions here, your hurt has lessened in any way about the conflict you identified, what idiomatic distance are you at now (compared to your answer to the second part of the fifth question) that shows you are distancing yourself from the conflict?

- What will you remember most from this set of questions that will help you in your efforts to gain distance from possible hurts in future conflicts? What conflict-masterful ways will you use to prevent another person from hurting you in future conflicts?

- What else occurs to you as you consider these questions?

- What insights do you have?

Just Because I Said It

In Adele's song "Rumor Has It," there is a line that goes, "Just 'cause I said it, don't mean that I meant it." This statement and its sentiment are relevant to what occurs in some of our interpersonal conflicts. That is, although we may intentionally want to hurt the other person, we often say things we do not mean. Our impulses may dictate our actions at times, and we react without thinking. We blurt out things we later regret, and stumble over later in our efforts to make amends.

We know intellectually that conflict mastery requires self-awareness, self-control, self-discipline, and self-regulation. However, until we get there, it is necessary to learn how to apply these competencies when tempers escalate and we risk losing our rationality. After the conflict, it may be too late to convince the other person that we did not mean what we said or did.

Learning proactive, conflict-masterful approaches to conflict includes exploring the occasions when we say things we do not mean. This helps us to understand what compels our specific reactions and the "disconnects" that emerge in these circumstances. As with the topics **Regrets After Conflict** and **Considering the Consequences of What We Say**, such an examination includes reflecting on our intentions and our hopes for the outcome.

This topic also explores the impulses that lead us to say things we later wish we could take back. The questions that follow will help those who routinely find themselves trying to apologize for words they did not mean. It is suggested that you focus on one situation initially and then repeat the questions for other scenarios to help identify recurring themes about this particular conflict response.

QUESTIONS

- When you consider a specific conflict situation, what exactly did you say that you did not mean?

- What motivated you to say what you did? What were you intending to accomplish by what you said?

- What were you feeling about the other person, and the conflict, at the time you said what you did not mean?

- What was the other person's reaction to what you said? What happened in the interaction after you said what you did? What was that like for you? From what you could observe and hear, what was it like for the other person?

- What ongoing recollection of this interaction is affecting you most now?

- As you look back on the conflict, what specifically kept you from holding back comments you did not mean?

- If you had it to do over again, what would you say or do instead?

- What themes from this and other conflicts might you identify, if any, that reflect the sorts of interactions, relationships, or other variables that result in your saying what you do not mean?

- What do you think makes it possible for you to say what you mean in some situations and not others? What are the differences and similarities? What have you learned in answering this question?

- In general, what might you do going forward to ensure that you say only what you mean when in conflict? What specifically do you intend to do next time to help you refrain from saying things that you do not mean? What other conflict-masterful approaches do you think are important for managing conflicts in this regard?

- What else occurs to you as you consider these questions?

- What insights do you have?

True or Not So True Conflict Story-Telling

Factors such as how offended we continue to feel after a conflict, what the outcome is, the impact on the relationship, and a host of other influences affect the "spin" we convey to others about what transpired. We speak truths and untruths. We may embellish our perspective on the situation and the relationship dynamic. We may also tend to play down our own contribution and exaggerate the other person's. Fact sometimes gets wound up in fiction as the space and time widen between the dispute and the present moment. (**Regrets After Conflict** and **Post-Conflict Guilt** also address what we convey to others about our conflicts.)

What we relate to ourselves and others about our conflicts also reflects such things as our individual resilience and subjective ways of managing our disputes and their aftermath. Though our perceptions are our realities, we have the choice post-conflict to own our truths and not alter them to make ourselves feel better, justify and defend ourselves, lay blame on the other person, and otherwise distort the interaction in our self-interest. Sometimes, though, we remain so entrenched in our own version of events that we lose some truths. And it may be that the truths we lose reflect the hopes we had about the interaction, or the parts we are ashamed of, or the pain we caused or experienced.

One aspect of developing conflict mastery is to think about what occurred in our disputes, and consider how our reality is different from the other person's and from that of others who might observe the interaction. And it helps to reflect on what our distorted or embellished stories represent. Being honest with ourselves about our part and what happened can be humbling, and it takes courage to go there. Thinking too about the differing perceptions we have on the issues and our contribution reminds us of our vulnerabilities and the places we go in our heart and mind to protect and defend ourselves or our viewpoints, to feel better, and to find our way through our conflicts.

The following questions will facilitate reflections to help open up some truths you may be denying. Bringing to mind a specific interaction also provides a context from which to learn and gain insights.

QUESTIONS

- What are the facts, as you perceive them, about what the other person said or did in the interaction that contributed to the conflict?

- If the other person listened to your description (your answer to the above question), with what is she or he likely to agree? With what is she or he likely to disagree? What might she or he add to your explanation of the facts?

- What are the facts, from your perspective, about what you said or did in that same interaction that may have contributed to the conflict?

- With what might the other person agree, if she or he heard your view of what you said or did (your answer to the previous question). With what might she or he not agree? What might she or he add to your description here?

- If a trusted friend observed what happened between you, what might she or he question about your version of events—specifically about what the other person said or did? What might she or he question about your version of what you said or did?

- What other facts might the trusted friend who observed the interaction add about what you said or did that is relevant to the conflict dynamic and its evolution? What might she or he add about what the other person said or did?

- If you have distorted, exaggerated, or denied some things you said or did, what might you be protecting? Or, what other reasons might you have had for changing the story—or not fully including some things you said or did?

- What, if anything, do you want to admit that you are ashamed or embarrassed about, or otherwise concerned about sharing, regarding the situation as you have described it so far?

- What else, if anything, do you know to be true that you might be hesitant to express about this conflict? If this question applies, what is the hesitation about? How might disclosing that information, and your answer to the previous question, change the perception of the conflict and your interaction with the other person?

- In general, what do you think the challenges are for some of us to acknowledge the whole truth about conflicts after they are over? In what ways does your answer apply to you, if it does, that you have not yet mentioned?

- What else occurs to you as you consider these questions?

- What insights do you have?

Mending Fences

After a conflict, some of us let go of feelings we experienced and the hurtful words said or exchanged. We sense that things are settled, and are relieved and move on. Sometimes, though, we may have some doubts and are unsure that matters are fully settled, and we find this uncertainty discomforting. We realize we want to ensure that the issues and the relationship are reconciled, and have a stronger sense of overall resolve. The expression "mending fences" has been used to describe this sort of objective—a common goal when we are in conflict with others. This is especially the case with people we care about and with whom we have ongoing relationships.

The expression "mending fences" may date back to the mid-17th century maxim, "Good fences make good neighbors."[2] Robert Frost used the phrase in his 1914 poem "Mending Wall" in relation to rebuilding previously good relationships.

The analogy of mending a fence, as it applies to making amends in conflict, provides a compelling visual with which to explore reconciling matters post-conflict. For instance, the success in re-establishing a durable relationship is likely to be short-lived if efforts to mend it are done half-heartedly, in haste, or without a solid ground and strong tools or materials. On the other hand, when efforts are made with the intention of rebuilding what was lost and restoring the relationship, the resulting structure stands on a more stable foundation. This point is also related to the discussion of positive conflict in Chapter 1.

If the expression "mending fences" resonates for you and applies to your goal of strengthening the post-conflict relationship, the following questions will facilitate that objective.

QUESTIONS

- When you consider a dispute in which you would like to reconcile the relationship with the other person, how does the expression "mending fences" apply?

- What specifically about the relationship do you sense is not quite mended as yet (if you did not answer this)? Why do you think that is so?

- What makes this relationship especially important to you? How might the other person respond if she or he heard your answer to this question? What do you hope the other person would say makes your relationship especially important to her or him?

- When the fences are mended between you and the other person, what do you want to feel about her or him that you do not feel now? What do you want to feel about yourself?

- What do you want the other person to think and feel about you when things are mended? What do you think needs to be said or done to make that happen?

- What do you think the other person may want to mend regarding the relationship that you have not referred to so far? What are your thoughts on that?

- What do you want to ensure happens in the process of mending fences that you have not referred to as yet?

- What do you want to ensure does *not* happen in the mending process?

- Figuratively speaking, what will the ground—on which the fence stands—consist of to ensure it is solid? What metaphorical tools will you use to ensure the fence is mended well and in a lasting way?

- What else about the mending fences metaphor resonates for you that you will carry forward in managing future conflicts in conflict-masterful ways?

- What else occurs to you as you consider these questions?

- What insights do you have?

Peeling Back the Onion

An onion is an apt metaphor to describe the many "layers" that comprise our disputes. For instance, the layers could represent our heart and brain, our spiritual being, and our body, all of which are affected when we are in conflict. Our personality, previous experiences in other disputes, and our conflict management style and habits also form layers. All of these aspects build on one another and every new conflict adds or supports another layer, making up the idiomatic onion that represents our conflict history.

By peeling back the layers and paying attention to the substance, we gain increased understanding of how we manage conflict and the specific dynamics that occur. We are then better able to increase our self-awareness and put ourselves in a place and space to be able to construct more effective ways of being, and to make the changes we want in our efforts to achieve conflict mastery.

To consider the metaphoric onion further, with increased conflict intelligence we discover how conflict, like onions, can add flavor to our lives and can even nurture us. We learn how to cut through them. We also accept that tears may come at times when we slice into onions. We realize we can grow onions, fry them, eat them, and throw them away.

After we have been in a dispute, it is a good time to peel back the layers of what the onion represents, to see what it is made of, to learn from it, and to concentrate our efforts on building conflict intelligence. The following questions facilitate such an exploration if this metaphor resonates for you as it applies to a particular situation. **The Conflict Iceberg** in Chapter 3 also discusses layers below the surface that are relevant here.

QUESTIONS

- What about the metaphor of an onion resonates most regarding how you managed a specific conflict?

- If you were to pull back the top five layers of that conflict, what would you find those are made of?

- How would you describe the layer(s) that had the most impact on you in this particular dispute?

- If you sliced through the onion, what might you find that represents the underlying seed that resulted in the conflict's growth? What else in your history of engaging in conflict influenced how you managed this one?

- What part of the onion's layers brings tears to your eyes specific to this conflict? What does your answer here say about what is important to you?

- What part of the conflict elicited a reaction in the other person that may represent one or more layers of her or his onion? What was that reaction? Which of her or his layers were you able to identify?

- What else did you become aware of, or were reminded of, during the conflict that reflects what is important to the other person?

- What part of the conflict has healthy, or potentially healthy, aspects for you and the relationship? What might help bring out those aspects?

- When you consider this conflict as an onion, in what ways does that help you reframe it? What learning have you gained from deconstructing your specific conflict with this set of questions that provides a different way of viewing it? What else is different now?

- Generally, what other vegetable might be a meaningful metaphor to represent conflict? Why is that so? Or, if not another vegetable, what object might provide an effective visual or other metaphoric way of describing what comprises conflict for you? How will that visual help you be more conflict masterful in future conflicts?

- What else occurs to you as you consider these questions?

- What insights do you have?

Were You Hearing?

When we continue to remain unsettled after our conflicts, we sometimes try to think through what was said to see if we can process what occurred that continues to lean on us. Sometimes, though, we are not willing to remember. Yet, niggling memories of bits and pieces of what happened may emerge, including unreconciled thoughts and emotions.

In the aftermath of conflict, our memory of the interaction sometimes gets in the way of moving on. Some details we heard may have seemed inconsequential at the time and so, we dismissed them. However, they may creep into our consciousness when we least expect it. Or, maybe we are trying not to retain certain things that were said out of a need to put things behind us. For instance, the other person may have spoken words we perceived as blameful and retaliatory, and we want to forget them. Or, we may have blocked what she or he said because it was unbelievable, too painful to hear, or too bizarre according to our version of the events. However, some things that are said in our conflicts may re-enter our awareness afterwards—and even a long time afterwards—much to our consternation.

There are times, too, when we do not fully hear what the other person said, and memory can be selective at the best of times. Sometimes, too, our voices dominate so that we do not hear what the other person is saying. A need to be right, to upstage, to challenge, or to win may also preclude our ability to listen and hear. We may have deliberately tried not to hear the other person's messages, and we may have been closed to perspectives different from our own.

The reality is that what is exchanged in a dispute is meaningful, even if it is painful to hear, and ultimately influences whether resolution and reconciliation are possible and sustainable. There may also be important lessons to learn about ourselves and the other person that we miss when we do not hear each other. It is true that some things are difficult to digest at the time. However, careful listening is a major hallmark in the quest for conflict mastery and integral to the concept of positive conflict (as discussed in Chapter 1). **Considering the Consequences of What We Say** is also relevant to this topic.

As discussed in Chapter 3: **When Silence Is Golden**, listening and hearing are complex proficiencies. For instance, it is important that our eyes—not just our ears—are engaged. It is also important to ensure that our empathy and compassion are tuned in. What is more, listening is about being present and attentive. It is also about not letting our own or the other person's emotions preclude us from taking in and interpreting each other's words and intent. It is about acknowledging to the other person that we hear what she or he is saying. To be able to move on after conflict, it helps to concentrate on—and not resist—what remains unprocessed about what we heard that keeps us planted in the past.

The questions in this topic invite those who continue to experience niggling and unclear thoughts and feelings after an interaction to focus, with intention, on what the other person said. They also ask you to contemplate whether what you conveyed was clearly heard, and what it takes to both hear and be heard.

QUESTIONS

- When you consider a specific altercation, what do you recall that the other person actually said (rather than your interpretation) that concerned or upset you? What surprised you about what the other person said? What hurt you that she or he said?

- What emotions did you hear and observe the other person express? What do you think was important to the other person that was contained in her or his words and expression of feelings? What did you hear she or he needed from you with respect to the situation?

- What messages did the other person not actually verbalize, but you interpreted from her or his words, actions, attitude, emotions, facial and body language, and so on? From what, specifically, did you interpret those messages? What other interpretations of those messages might be possible?

- What did you want to hear that you did not? You may have a recollection of some things the other person said, but they were difficult to take in at the time. If that is possible, what were those things? What else might you have missed hearing that she or he conveyed?

- What did you hear the other person say—directly or by interpretation—that contains one or more valid points that you intend to consider in an effort to reconcile your differences (if this is what you want to do)?

- What did you say to the other person that acknowledged to her or him that you heard what was said? If you said nothing, what might you have said?

- What did you need from the other person but you did not say so? What else was important to you that you did not express? Why did you not say those things? Or, if you said what you needed, or something else important that you do not think the other person heard, what gives you that impression (if this point is applicable)?

- What did you hear yourself say that hurt the other person?

- What do you wish the other person had acknowledged about what you said?

- What do you realize about yourself from this situation that you want to work on in your quest for conflict mastery with respect to being heard more effectively when in conflict? What conflict-masterful approaches would you like to focus on going forward, to be able to listen and hear more effectively in contentious situations?

- What else occurs to you as you consider these questions?

- What insights do you have?

"Woulda Coulda Shoulda"

The expression "woulda coulda shoulda" is sometimes said after a conflict when lamenting something we said or did, or did not say or do, and we are annoyed with ourselves that we did not handle the situation more effectively. According to WiseGeek: "For many people, there is a clear distinction between what actually happened and what they *wished* would have happened in a given situation. Sometimes, people realize a number of options they could have or should have taken instead of the action they actually took."[3]

The time and energy wasted after some conflicts replete with "woulda coulda shoulda" language can be all-consuming. Commonly, our recriminations also add to continued tension between the other person and us. Even criticizing ourselves for things we did not say or do when we had the opportunity creates discomfort for those who listen to our plaints. It is an understatement to say it is easier in hindsight to consider what may have been more constructive ways to manage a conflict.

Why do some of us engage in "woulda coulda shoulda" complaints? Previous topics in this chapter—**Post-Conflict Agony**, **Regrets After Conflict**, and **Second-Guessing the Conflict**—suggest a number of reasons such as unresolved issues, lack of reconciliation of the relationship, and continuing emotional investment in what occurred. Wishing we had defended ourselves and expressed something of major importance that we did not express are also high on the list of reasons we agonize after conflict. These and other reasons may vary from situation to situation, though certain patterns may be evident for some of us.

When self-blame prevails, it is an opportune time to assess the "woulda coulda shouldas" of the situation. By doing so we can check out the validity of saying or doing what we wished we had. We can also consider the learning to be gained so that we do not end up with regrets after future conflicts. The following questions aim to facilitate such an exercise.

QUESTIONS

- When you consider a conflict about which you continue to blame yourself for some aspects, what is the "woulda" part?

- What information, knowledge, or skill, if you had it, might have helped you with the "woulda" part of the situation? What impact might those factors (your answer here) have had on how matters unfolded? How may you have obtained that information, knowledge, or skill?

- What is the action you "coulda" taken? Why did you not do that? If you had taken that action, what do you believe would have happened that is different from what did occur?

- What other "couldas" come to mind about this conflict?

- What do you think you "shoulda" said or done instead or differently? What stopped you? What other "shouldas" are on your mind?

- If you did say or do what you think you "shoulda," what different outcome may there be?

- In what other ways are you blaming yourself about this particular interaction? How is that self-blame affecting you? How does it affect the relationship with the other person?

- In what ways does self-blame and the "woulda coulda shoulda" wishes keep you engaged in the dispute? What may self-blame accomplish that you do not want to let go of—at least not yet?

- How much do you want to stop blaming yourself on a scale of 1 to 5, 5 being "very much" and 1 being "not at all"? If you answered 5, what do you need to be able to stop blaming yourself? If you answered less than 5, what does your rating mean in the context of this situation?

- What lessons are you learning from analyzing this past conflict in this way? What do you intend to do differently that will change the way you approach future conflicts based on your learning here?

- What else occurs to you as you consider these questions?

- What insights do you have?

That's Just Not Fair

One of the common refrains that occurs in conflict is, "that's just not fair." It may be our response to an action that we view as undermining something important to us. It may be our reaction to a decision made or position taken on a matter with which we disagree, or a rule, policy, or procedure that we experience as oppressive or threatening and that has resulted in an altercation. It may be a perception that another person is being arbitrary, unthinking, obstinate, and so on. It may be that someone has achieved something we believe we are entitled to have. Or, it may be that the other person in a dispute expects us to concede something we do not want to concede. These and other examples of how we perceive unfairness have an impact on the nature of our conflicts, how we process them, and whether we ultimately reconcile our differences.

Fairness, like other values, is subjective and contextual, and is derived from our personal conditioning, culture, and other influences. As with many other values, there does not usually appear to be degrees of fairness. Rather, it commonly seems things are perceived as either fair or unfair. In any case, differing interpretations of what constitutes fairness, and the related polarization, often result in conflict.

The following set of questions helps to deconstruct the concept of fairness as it emerged during a past conflict.

QUESTIONS

- Generally, what for you makes a statement, decision, action, and so on fair? What makes something unfair that may not be inherently included in your answer?

- When you consider a conflict you had with someone who did or said something you thought unfair, what was that? What made it unfair in your view? How is what you consider unfair affecting you?

- On a scale of 1 to 5, 5 being "very fair" and 1 being "very unfair," what rating do you give the level of fairness of the other person's actions or statements in this situation? What made it so as compared to a lower rating, if this is applicable? What made it so as compared to a higher rating, if this is applicable?

- What had been your expectation of the other person in the conflict situation? What let you down most about what she or he said or did, or did not say or do (if you did not answer this previously)?

- From what you can tell or know, what reasons might the other person provide to explain how her or his actions or words were fair? What, if anything, about these possible explanations sounds plausible to you?

- If, by chance, in some other situation you have said or done something similar to what this person said or did, what other reasons might emerge from considering your own experience?

- What might the other person have said or done differently in this situation for you to have experienced what she or he said or did as fair or fairer? What specifically makes that fairer?

- If it were you in the other person's place in the same situation, what would you have said or done differently to have been, or been perceived as, fairer? What might be considered unfair about that situation? Again, if it were you in the other person's place, what might you have done similarly or the same as her or him?

- Now that you have thought about this conflict further, what do you realize you do *not* know about the other person and the situation that might be helpful before deciding how to manage it and the impact of what you determine as unfair?

- How do these questions shift, if at all, the way you perceive the other person's fairness in this situation? In any case, in what conflict-masterful ways will you proceed with this conflict?

- What else occurs to you as you consider these questions?

- What insights do you have?

Forgetting About "It"

Many of us store, at some level of consciousness, the emotional repercussions and the impressions we make about the other person during a conflict. Certain conflicts leave scars that are difficult to erase from our memory. What we hold onto is meaningful, because our lingering feelings and thoughts reflect things that are important to us and that remain unresolved. **Peeling Back the Onion** in this chapter also speaks to the layers of conflict that build up over time from repeated conflicts.

Ongoing emotional reactions to our conflicts stay with us in various ways. They may show up again in situations with the same person or with others when similar dynamics arise. Or, we may displace our emotions onto bystanders or on irrelevant issues that provoke us. Sometimes we intentionally hold onto things we do not want to let go of to protect ourselves in case of future challenges with the other person. As a consequence of these possible repercussions, in relation to this person and sometimes others, we may remain untrusting, resentful, guarded, cautious, and defensive.

Intertwined with moving forward after a conflict is identifying the "it" that remains for some of us that we are not forgetting. For instance, is the "it" the ongoing thoughts and feelings that are consuming us? Is "it" what the other person said or did? Is "it" what we said or did? Is "it" the fact of being in conflict at all? Is "it" that we treated each other poorly or acted in uncharacteristic ways? Or is "it" hard to identify?

Unless we figure out what continues to ail us after our interpersonal disputes, we will lug the baggage around with us. And, as in **The Weight of Conflict**, it often feels a heavy load to carry the thoughts and feelings we cannot seem to reconcile. Naming and acknowledging just what "it" is that we warehouse, then, is an important aspect of conflict mastery that entails unpacking the load we continue to carry to be able to move forward.

The line of inquiry here expands on **Gaining Distance from Hurts** and anticipates **Letting Go**, which also discuss some elements of this aspect of conflict. To explore this topic, it helps to bring to mind a dispute and something about it that you cannot forget.

QUESTIONS

- What happened in the specific dispute you brought to mind? What is the "it" you are not forgetting about what happened? If there is more than one "it," what are they? (You may want to use the plural "them" in answering these questions.)

- What is particularly significant about "it" for you (your answer to the previous question)? What is the impact on you about not forgetting "it"?

- If the other person is aware of the "it" you are not forgetting, what impact is that having on her or him, from what you can tell? What is the impact of not forgetting "it" on how you two are now interacting?

- In what ways might you be taking out your feelings on others because of the "it" you are not forgetting?

- If you could forget "it," how would that change matters between you and the other person? How might you feel about her or him that you do not right now? How might you feel differently within yourself?

- What might you lose if you forget "it"? What are you gaining by not forgetting "it"? What are any other positive outcomes of not forgetting "it"?

- If you do not (want to) forget "it," what will that mean for the relationship? How is that an outcome you can live with? How is it not a result you can live with?

- If not forgetting "it" has negative consequences for the relationship and you do not want that, what are your options?

- The memory you have of "it" in this situation may also reflect something you are not forgetting about a previous situation with the same person or someone else. If that is the case, what theme(s) are you recognizing?

- What learning do you want to hold onto about "it" that will help you strengthen your conflict intelligence—and the way you manage future conflicts?

- What else occurs to you as you consider these questions?

- What insights do you have?

Receiving Apologies

It often happens after an interpersonal dispute that one or both of us apologize for what we said or did. We may realize our actions were not warranted and that we said something that offended the other person. We may have acted out of malice and in mean-spirited ways. As in **Regrets After Conflict**, **Post-Conflict Guilt**, and **"Woulda Coulda Shoulda,"** the list of things about which we experience remorse after our conflicts can be long at times.

The thing is, sometimes after a conflict we may not be quite ready to extend an apology or to receive one. Sometimes we find something said or done to be unforgivable. Sometimes we accept an apology or deliver one and we do not really mean it. Sometimes we mean an apology and it is not well received by the other person. Sometimes we receive an apology but we do not forgive the person. These and other factors figure into whether and when we decide to apologize and accept someone else's apology.

Whether we apologize or the other person does or we both do, we have subjective ideas regarding what constitutes a sincere apology. Tone of voice, words used, timing, degree of sincerity perceived, and body language are just some of the variables we each contemplate.

The following questions ask you to consider what has worked for you as the recipient of an apology after a conflict. The questions are also helpful to consider important factors when making your own apologies, a topic that is expanded on in **Delivering an Apology** and the following one, **About Forgiving**.

QUESTIONS

- When people apologize to you and you find the apology effective, what are they saying or doing that makes it so?

- How else do you describe the best ingredients of an effective apology when someone is making one to you?

- How does it feel when someone apologizes and you are not quite ready to accept the apology?

- What conflict-masterful practices do you use regarding how you respond when you are not ready to receive an apology? Or, if you do not currently have specific practices in this regard, what ones occur to you as effective ways to respond?

- Under what circumstances have you found it most difficult to accept an apology? Under what circumstances is it easiest?

- When you consider a specific situation in which you did not accept an apology given, what was the reason? What was that like for you? How did the other person respond?

- What positive outcomes came from not accepting the apology? What was not so positive?

- What motivates you to say "apology accepted" (or something else that indicates your acceptance) when you do not really mean it, if that has happened?

- What is it like for you when you say you accept an apology but you do not forgive the person, if that has happened?

- Over time—whether or not you forgive the other person—what have you learned to be your most conflict-masterful ways of receiving apologies? What makes them so? What emotions or other indicators do you experience when you are given an apology that you receive well?

- What else occurs to you as you consider these questions?

- What insights do you have?

Delivering an Apology

This further set of questions on the topic of apologies is about delivering them. Depending on a range of circumstances, we do not always know whether our apology will be received well and if the other person is ready and willing to listen and to forgive us. Or, we do not always know if we are ready and sincerely wanting to apologize. We may just say we are sorry because we think that is expected. Or, someone—even the other person—tells us to apologize though we are not certain we want to, at least not at the time.

As with other considerations in post-conflict initiatives, our intentions and the outcome we want, the other person's readiness and our own, the degree of offense taken, our respective contributions to the discord, and our lingering perceptions and distress about what happened, among other factors, influence both the act of apologizing and the willingness to forgive. (**About Forgiving** is the next topic.)

With respect to delivering an apology, it helps to give some time and energy to consider why we are thinking about giving an apology, what we are sorry for, and for what we want forgiveness. It also helps to reflect on what we want to say, and how, before proceeding, and to prepare for the possible responses. The following questions help explore an apology you are thinking about giving.

QUESTIONS

- When you consider a particular situation in which you are deciding whether to extend an apology for something you said or did, why do you think an apology is warranted?

- If you do not think an apology is warranted, why is that the case? What is to be gained by apologizing when you do not think an apology is warranted? What is to be lost by doing so? What factors will you consider in your decision about whether to proceed with an apology if you do not think it is warranted?

- What is the outcome you hope to achieve if you decide to proceed with your apology? What else do you intend to happen by apologizing?

- What do you want to say in your apology? What sentiments will you convey that you believe are appropriate and are likely to be well received?

- What do you think the other person may expect or want you to acknowledge and apologize for, if anything (that you have not mentioned in response to the questions so far)? If you do not want to apologize for what she or he might expect or want, how will you handle the conversation in that regard?

- What will you *not* say in your apology because it might lead to a negative reaction you do not want to evoke?

- What tone of voice do you plan to use? What body language is likely to be effective if you extend the apology in person? If you use other means and you and the other person do not see each other directly, what do you want to keep in mind about your communications?

- What do you want to be most prepared for that the other person might say or do when you deliver your apology? How do you intend to respond if the other person does not accept your apology?

- If you were the other person on the receiving end of your intended apology, what would motivate you to accept it?

- What ways have others apologized to you that have been most effective? When you have effectively apologized before, what have you said or done? What other conflict-masterful approaches do you plan to use in the apology you are going to deliver?

- What else occurs to you as you consider these questions?

- What insights do you have?

About Forgiving

In interpersonal conflicts, apologies are expressed for things said or done or not said or done, and one or both people may deliver them. Apologizing may be stated as briefly as: "Forgive me"; "I apologize"; "I was an idiot"; "You didn't deserve what I said"; "I was wrong"; "I didn't mean it"; or "Will you please forgive me?" Others of us elaborate on what we identify as requiring forgiveness to let the other person know we acknowledge the words or actions that were hurtful, inappropriate, and so on. Other people combine these approaches to convey apologies.

Sometimes requests for forgiveness come out automatically, like an impulsive or rote plea that seems to be uttered with minimal thought and sincerity. When we are on the receiving end of a quick "I'm sorry," some of us just as automatically and quickly respond, "That's okay," or "Never mind," or "Thanks apology accepted." However, forgiving is not necessarily the immediate response or reflect what we are feeling. Other times, requests for forgiveness come to us after feelings have settled and we have had time to contemplate the fallout and our part in it. We are not necessarily in a more accepting frame of mind in either case, though we may be.

There is no absolute rule about forgiving, and some of us find it easier to accept an apology and forgive than others. Many variables go into our subjective determinations as to whether an apology is acceptable. For instance, we may not believe or trust the other person. Maybe we are fed up with the frequency of her or his offending words or actions, and a continual demonstration of an attitude that is abrasive, judgmental, disconcerting, righteous, and so on. Maybe too, we are not willing to forgive because of unprocessed and unresolved thoughts and feelings about the conflict. Maybe we experience a sense of power or vindication by denying the other person our forgiveness. Maybe we are so deeply hurt we are not ready and willing to forgive. Or, perhaps, we have not forgiven ourselves for something.

These and other factors, including the nature and duration of the relationship, influence our motivation and readiness to forgive, and to let go of certain emotions about what occurred between us. However, there are times that forgiving is not something we are prepared to consider because some things are unforgiveable to us, and no amount of apologizing will repair the pain and indelible marks left behind.

Though it is liberating for many of us—and reportedly beneficial to our health and well-being—to forgive, we all have different thresholds about what is forgivable and what is not. It is therefore presumptuous to expect ourselves—and others—to necessarily forgive in response to apologies, however they are delivered. This is so regardless of how genuine the other person is, or we are, in the apology.

If you are not forgiving someone despite her or his apology after a specific conflict, the following questions are for you. If you have apologized to someone who is not forgiving you, consider reversing the questions to the extent they apply. (The previous two topics—**Delivering an Apology** and **Receiving Apologies**—are also relevant to the content here.)

QUESTIONS

- What did the other person say or do in the conflict that you do not want, or are not prepared, to forgive despite her or his apology? What impact is not forgiving having on the relationship? What impact is not forgiving having on you?

- What was not effective about the other person's apology, if anything? What was effective about it, if anything?

- What would you have liked the other person to have said or done differently that might have changed your response to the apology? Or, what could she or he have said or done in addition to the apology?

- What are you accomplishing by not forgiving? What makes that especially important to you?

- How much do you want the relationship to be healed on a scale of 1 to 5, 5 being "very much" and 1 being "not at all"? What might your answer reflect that you have not forgiven? What else does your rating mean?

- What might be different for you when you forgive the other person, if you do? What do you suppose it will be like for the other person? How about the relationship?

- For what, if anything, are you not forgiving yourself?

- Forgiving may not be what you want to do. If that is the case, what does this mean going forward?

- If you want to forgive the other person, what has to happen before you might be ready to do so?

- What signs will there be when you know you have forgiven the other person?

- What else occurs to you as you consider these questions?

- What insights do you have?

Letting Go

Letting go essentially means that we move on after an interpersonal conflict without ongoing blame and regret. This may be whether or not the issues in dispute are resolved to our satisfaction. Letting go also means we do not continue to dwell on what we did not get that we wanted, or on what was said or done or not said or done. It means we do not otherwise remain preoccupied with what occurred during the conflict interaction or the negative emotions generated within it.

Further, letting go means we do not let the dynamic adversely affect our ongoing relationship with the other person. It means, too, that we do not hold onto memories of the other person's conduct, or our own, in unforgiving and resentful ways. It means what was said and done does not get regurgitated at a future time, and that we do not have a continuing need to rail against the other person to friends and family. The next topic—**Bouncing Back**—also discusses more relevant variables.

Many circumstances influence whether and how we move past our conflicts, and also the speed with which we do so. Certain people, kinds of disputes, ways of interacting, times of day, moods, and other variables affect how we react post-conflict. These are just some of the aspects of conflict that have an impact on how we process what occurred. And we do so in accordance with our individual ways of managing discord and ourselves within it. (See also **Forgetting About "It," Receiving Apologies**, and **About Forgiving**.)

It is sometimes challenging to let go of the emotional pain some conflicts engender. However, this series of questions provide an opportunity to consider various aspects of letting go, to see if they apply to a specific dispute you continue to hold onto.

QUESTIONS

- What are you not letting go of in your particular dispute? More specifically, what is it about those things (that thing) that makes it difficult for you to let go?

- What does holding on to those things (that thing) satisfy—such as a need, hope, or expectation? (It helps to be specific in response to this question.)

- What do you want to have happen in this situation or relationship that may be achieved by holding on?

- What do you imagine happening between you and the other person if you do not let go? What is acceptable about that result? What is not acceptable?

- If you let go, what is the worst-case scenario you imagine? What is acceptable about that result that you are willing to live with? What is not acceptable about that result? What is the best-case scenario, if you let go of what you are holding onto?

- It is possible that you do not want to let go of what you are holding onto. What is it like for you when you consider this possibility? It is possible you are not quite ready to let go. If that is the case, what will indicate you are ready?

- If you decide to begin the process of letting go, what part of what happened would you let go of first? What is it like for you just thinking of beginning to let go of a part of what is affecting you?

- If you picture yourself a year from now, how do you want to feel about this conflict? What do you want to feel about the other person? What sort of relationship do you want to have with her or him?

- What do you want to be holding onto about the conflict a year from now? What do you want to have let go of? What will it take to achieve the things you answered in these and the previous questions that you want a year from now?

- What, if anything, are you thinking now about the idea of letting go that might be different from when you started to answer this set of questions?

- What else occurs to you as you consider these questions?

- What insights do you have?

Bouncing Back

Some of us bounce back quicker than others after interpersonal conflicts, and there are lots of reasons for that. Besides unresolved issues and emotions, other variables that influence our resilience include how we generally manage stress, our pessimistic or optimistic approaches to life, the intensity of lingering feelings, and how we are processing them. Other relevant factors include our physical well-being and general health and happiness.

What does it mean to bounce back from interpersonal conflicts? In addition to the variables referred to in **Letting Go**, the following signs are other examples that reflect elements of conflict intelligence and mastery. We regain our equilibrium, which may have been lost during a dispute; we accept that we did the best we could, or even if we did not, we are prepared to acknowledge that to ourselves and the other person; we do not let the interaction prey on us and taint the ongoing relationship; we do not hold a grudge against the other person; we forgive ourselves; we are not preoccupied with regrets about what we "should" have done; we move on; and we are grateful for the learning and intend to apply it in future conflicts.

When, after a conflict, we feel limited in our ability to bounce back in one or more of these and other ways, it is an opportune time to explore why that is the case. By doing so, we are better able to identify the choices we have about how to interact more effectively before and during conflict, and the skills that we need to strengthen further. We consider, too, what we need to learn so that we will not repeat behaviors that do not serve us well. And we examine what else keeps us from being resilient post-conflict.

If bouncing back is a challenge for you, the next series of questions are ones to consider. The questions in **"Woulda Coulda Shoulda"** and **Letting Go** are also helpful to answer in combination with these.

QUESTIONS

- About what specifically are you not being, or feeling, resilient regarding a past dispute?

- What are the things that continue to bother you most? What is it about those things that is having a negative impact on you?

- If you were bouncing back, what do you expect you would you be feeling, saying, and doing that you are not right now? What else would be different for you if you bounced back from that situation?

- How would being different in the way you just described affect your relationship with the other person? What would be different about your relationship with yourself?

- When you think about the expression "bouncing back" in relation to this dispute, what will you be bouncing back from? What, specifically, would you be bouncing to?

- What do you think will propel you to bounce back effectively in the way you want? How might you influence that happening?

- What positive things did you learn about yourself in the dispute that may help you bounce back? What did you learn about the other person that might help?

- What did you realize from how you interacted in this dispute that you do not want to repeat in future conflicts?

- How will you apply your learning from this dispute to facilitate your resilience in future conflicts?

- What skills do you want to hone to help you bounce back in this conflict and future conflicts?

- What else occurs to you as you consider these questions?

- What insights do you have?

Taking Stock

After a conflict is over, it helps to take stock. One relevant definition of this idiom is "to think carefully about a situation or event and form an opinion about it, so that you can decide what to do."[4] Another is "to assess a situation, to conduct a personal inventory of one's beliefs and values, etc."[5]

Besides the things we hold onto post-conflict—such as those described in **Letting Go** and **Bouncing Back**—it frequently happens in the aftermath of our disputes that we revisit what occurred, even when we do not want to. Memories of what we or the other person said or did sometimes spontaneously pop up. Or, we recall a feeling we had at the time, which then comes back and even sticks with us for a while. Or, we may share our narrative of the situation, as we perceived and experienced it, with friends or family, keeping the story and the emotions alive.

An inventory of sorts seems to unfold when any of these and other post-conflict thoughts and feelings occur. Examining what contributed to the evolution of the conflict in the first place, and taking a close look at why the remaining bruises are not fading, often helps in the learning to carry forward. This does not mean going back in time to blame others or ourselves. Rather, it means reflecting on the knowledge and understanding we now have so that we do not repeat counterproductive behaviors in the future.

To take stock with conflict intelligence also means to consider what else we gained from a dispute, including a better understanding about what is meaningful to us and the other person, individually and collectively. What more we need to be able to reconcile the conflict, and our feelings about it and the other person, is similarly important. We may realize there are patterns we are repeating about how we interact that warrant our attention, too.

Taking an inventory of our conflicts may lead to a discussion with the other person, or to some soul-searching, that helps us process the interaction and facilitate our ongoing quest for conflict mastery. Post-conflict reflections also alert us to the skills that require strengthening, and what else we intend to work on going forward.

The following questions will help you to take stock of a particular conflict and consider what will facilitate your efforts to become more conflict masterful. Engaging in this exercise—and also repeating the questions for other conflicts you are still ruminating on—will help to identify possible patterns worth exploring.

QUESTIONS

- What happened in a specific conflict that you want to take stock of? What specific-ally do you want to take stock of (if you did not refer to that in response to the previous question), such as what provoked conflict for you, some other specific part of the interaction, your ongoing emotions or thoughts, and so on? Why did you select that or those parts of the conflict in particular?

- What did you do well that was helpful in the conflict (such as how you interacted, listened, and so on)? What could you have done more effectively?

- To what did you react most negatively that the other person said or did in the conflict being discussed? How did you react? What are the specific reasons for your reaction?

- Which of your beliefs, needs, and values come to the surface as you consider the reasons you referred to in the previous question? What does this inventory (of your beliefs, needs, and values) raise about what is important to you?

- What do you need to reconcile with the other person before you are able to move forward? What remains unreconciled in yourself that precludes forward movement?

- How did you contribute to the conflict (other than what you might have mentioned so far) that may reflect a pattern you repeat when in conflict?

- What themes are emerging for you, if any, as you take stock of this conflict now, such as patterns you want to change? Consider, for instance, what repeatedly evokes reactions in you, what those reactions are, habitual ways of defending yourself, and so on.

- What else did you learn about yourself in the conflict that you want to remember going forward?

- What specific skills or knowledge do you intend to develop further?

- What is different in your thinking about the conflict now from when you started this set of questions about the act of taking stock? What stands out as your biggest learning on this topic?

- What else occurs to you as you consider these questions?

- What insights do you have?

Notes

Chapter One: Important Considerations About Questions, Conflict, and Conflict Mastery

1. Examples of other books about this subject: Fredrike Bannink, *Handbook of Solution-Focused Conflict Management* (Hogrefe Publishing, 2010); Marilee Adams, PhD, *Change Your Questions, Change Your Life: 10 Powerful Tools for Life and Work* (Berrett-Koehler Publishers, 2009); Tony Stolzfus, *Coaching Questions: A Coach's Guide to Powerful Asking Skills* (Tony Stolzfus, www.coach22.com, 2008); Fredrike Bannink, *1001 Solution-Focused Questions: Handbook for Solution-Focused Interviewing* (Pearson Assessment and Information, 2006); Dorothy Strachan, *Making Questions Work: A Guide to How and What to Ask for Facilitators, Consultants, Managers, Coaches and Educators* (John Wiley & Sons, 2006); Byron Katie, *Loving What Is: How Four Questions Can Change Your Life* (Harmony, 2002); Dorothy Strachan, *Questions That Work: A Resource for Facilitators* (ST Press, 2001); Brian Stanfield, General Editor for The Canadian Institute of Cultural Affairs, *The Art of Focused Conversation: 100 Ways to Access Group Wisdom in the Workplace* (New Society Publishers, 2000); Marilee Goldberg, *The Art of the Question: A Guide to Short-Term Question-Centered Therapy* (John Wiley & Sons, 1998).

2. ConflictMastery™ Quest(ions) Blog: http://www.cinergycoaching.com/blog.

3. Craig E. Runde and Tim A. Flanagan, *Becoming a Conflict Competent Leader: How You and Your Organization Can Manage Conflict Effectively* (San Francisco: Jossey-Bass, 2007), 22. Initially derived from the definition by Sal Capobianco, Mark Davis, and Linda Kraus, *Conflict Dynamics Profile* (St. Petersburg, FL: Eckerd College Leadership Development Institute, 1999).

4. Daniel Dana, *Managing Differences: How to Build Better Relationships at Work & Home* (Prairie Village, KS: MTI Publications, 2005), 224.

5. Kenneth Cloke, *The Crossroads of Conflict: A Journey into the Heart of Dispute Resolution* (California: Janis Publications Inc., 2006), 18.

6. Cheryl Picard and Marnie Jull, *Learning Through Deepening Conversations: A Key Strategy of Insight Mediation* (Conflict Resolution Quarterly, Vol. 29, No. 2, Winter 2011), 152.

7. Several references that analyze the evolution of conflict include: Cinnie Noble, *Conflict Management Coaching: The CINERGY™ Model* (CINERGY™ Coaching, www.cinergycoaching.com, 2012), 71; Kenneth R. Melchin and Cheryl A. Picard, *Transforming Conflict Through Insight* (Toronto: University of Toronto Press, 2008); Gary T. Furlong, *The Conflict Resolution Toolbox: Models and Maps for Analyzing, Diagnosing, and Resolving Conflict* (Toronto: John Wiley & Sons Canada, 2005); Christopher W. Moore, *The Mediation Process: Practical Strategies for Resolving Conflict*, 3rd ed. (San Francisco: Jossey-Bass, 2003); Bernard S. Mayer, *The Dynamics of Conflict Resolution: A Practitioner's Guide* (San Francisco: Jossey-Bass, 2000); and Chris Argyris, *Overcoming Organizational Defenses: Facilitating Organizational Learning* (Englewood Cliffs, NJ: Prentice Hall, 1990).

8. "Conflict occurs when we perceive one or more of our values, needs, and/or aspects of our identity is being challenged, threatened, or undermined by another person." Cinnie Noble, *Conflict Management Coaching: The CINERGY™ Model* (CINERGY™ Coaching, www.cinergycoaching.com/conflict-management-coaching-book, 2012), 50.

9. See more in Cinnie Noble, "The 'Fear Factor' and Conflict" (http://www.mediate.com/articles/NobleC12.cfm, August 2013).

10. *Ibid.*

11. David Whyte, *Everything is Waiting for You* (Many Rivers Press, 2007), http://www.davidwhyte.com.

12. From the quotation by American psychologist Wayne Dyer: https://www.youtube.com/watch?v=urQPraeeY0w.

Chapter Two: Before Conflict

1. http://www.phrases.org.uk/meanings/23400.html

2. http://en.wikipedia.org/wiki/Chip_on_your_shoulder

3. http://en.wikipedia.org/wiki/Cold_shoulder

4. Charles Hodgson, *Carnal Knowledge: A Navel Gazer's Dictionary of Anatomy, Etymology, and Trivia* (New York: Macmillan/St. Martin's Press, 2007, p. 272).

5. John Jamieson, John Johnstone, and John Longmuir, *Jamieson's Dictionary of the Scottish Language* (Edinburgh: W.P. Nimmo, 1867, p. 635).

6. http://www.phrases.org.uk/meanings/295700.html

7. http://en.wikipedia.org/wiki/Making_a_mountain_out_of_a_molehill

8. http://en.wikipedia.org/wiki/Reasonable_doubt

Chapter Three: During Conflict

1. See, for example, Kenneth Cloke and Joan Goldsmith, *Resolving Conflicts at Work: A Complete Guide for Everyone on the Job* (Hoboken, NJ: Jossey-Bass, 2000, p. 114).

2. http://en.wikipedia.org/wiki/Rumi

3. http://www.phrases.org.uk/meanings/sticks-and-stones-may-break-my-bones.html

4. http://www.chacha.com/question/who-said-'when-you-throw-dirt,-you-lose-ground'

5. https://ca.answers.yahoo.com/question/index?qid=20080331140344AAIuD7D

6. http://www.thefreedictionary.com/rev

7. http://www.phrases.org.uk/meanings/296600.html

8. http://idioms.thefreedictionary.com/put+nose+out+of+joint

9. http://en.wiktionary.org/wiki/walk_a_mile_in_someone's_shoes

10. http://en.wikipedia.org/wiki/Elephant_in_the_room

11. http://phrases.org.uk/meanings/silence-is-golden.html

12. http://www.thefreedictionary.com/silent+treatment

13. http://en.wikipedia.org/wiki/Straw_that_broke_the_camel's_back

Chapter 4: After Conflict

1. http://en.wikipedia.org/wiki/Guilt_(emotion)

2. http://phrases.org.uk/meanings/mend-fences.html

3. http://www.wisegeek.org/what-does-woulda-coulda-shoulda-mean.htm

4. http://dictionary.cambridge.org/dictionary/british/take-stock

5. http://www.usingenglish.com/reference/idioms/take+stock.html

OUR WORKSHOPS

Conflict Mastery

We offer Conflict Mastery workshops for coaches, leaders, mediators, HR professionals, and others who work with people in conflict and want to strengthen your conflict intelligence and mastery.

In this workshop participants will:

- learn more about conflict and its underpinnings
- examine your destructive and constructive responses to conflict, according to the Conflict Dynamics Profile® (www.conflictdynamics.org)
- gain insights into your responses to conflict that may adversely affect your professional effectiveness
- consider your choices for managing conflict differently
- make a plan for shifting unproductive conflict habits and strengthening your conflict intelligence.

www.conflictmastery.com

Conflict Management Coaching

Conflict management coaching, also known as conflict coaching, is a specialized niche in the field of coaching and conflict management. It is a one-on-one technique, in which a trained coach assists people to manage their disputes effectively and to enhance their conflict management skills. This process has wide application in the organizational context, and also for coaching individuals to participate in mediation, negotiation, and relational conflict. CINERGY® Coaching provides one-on-one conflict management coaching, and we also conduct workshops to teach others to coach using our methodology.

In the workshops participants gain:

- the theory, principles and methods specific to the CINERGY® model of conflict management coaching
- an understanding of the types of skills required to provide conflict management coaching
- experience with the coaching model as a coach, 'client' and observer

- knowledge of the many applications of this technique
- suggested documents and information about the logistics of conflict management coaching

Book: *Conflict Management Coaching: The CINERGY™ Model* by Cinnie Noble at http://www.cinergycoaching.com/conflict-management-coaching-book

Our training is conducted by telecourse, webinar, and face-to-face workshops around the world.

www.cinergycoaching.com

Please feel free to contact author Cinnie Noble, Founder of CINERGY® Coaching, if you are interested in Conflict Mastery or Conflict Management Coaching workshops. Email: cinnie@cinergycoaching.com

Other Books by Cinnie Noble

Conflict Mastery: Questions to Guide You, November 2014

Conflict Management Coaching: The CINERGY™ Model, Amazon.com, October 2011 (http://www.cinergycoaching.com/conflict-management-coaching-book)

Co-author with Ed Modell and Diane Brennan of a chapter entitled "Conflict Management" in L. Wildflower and D. Brennan, *The Handbook of Knowledge-Based Coaching*, Jossey-Bass, 2011

Family Mediation: A Guide for Lawyers, Canada Law Book, May 1999

Mediation Advocacy: Effective Client Representation in Mediation Proceedings, Emond Montgomery, 1998 (with co-authors Leslie Dizgun and Paul Emond)

Handi-Travel: A Resource Book for Disabled and Elderly Travellers, Canadian Rehabilitation Council for the Disabled, 1985 (1st edition) and 1987 (2nd edition)

The Disabled Traveller, Canadian Institute of Travel Counsellors, 1991 (an update of the book entitled *The Handicapped Traveller*)

The Handicapped Traveller: A Guidebook for Travel Counsellors, Canadian Institute of Travel Counsellors, 1982

For articles on conflict management and coaching, go to:
http://www.cinergycoaching.com/articles

Free Resources from CINERGY® Coaching

Self-assessment tools are helpful ways to gain an awareness of ourselves when it comes to engaging in conflict.

CINERGY® Coaching provides the following to you at no cost:

- Conflict Intelligence Self-Assessment
- Conflict Resilience Quotient

http://www.cinergycoaching.com/resources/self-assessment-tools

17271514R00169

Made in the USA
Middletown, DE
16 January 2015